The Christian Church has always [...] community. If God is to stir the slu[...] in the West our passion for mis[...] Mackay's straightforward, easy to read, and quite convincing work might well be used to awaken many to the real issues of modern missions.

John H. Armstrong
President, Reformation & Revival Ministries
Carol Stream, Illinois

In a day when so much writing on world mission is characterised by wishful thinking and fanciful speculation, *Global Warning* is welcome for its author's unequivocal commitment to biblical truth, and evident passion for the task of world evangelisation.

Rev. John Brand,
U.K. Director,
Africa Inland Mission International

When at the start of this millennium a Christian TV station can be fined £20,000 by the Independent Television Commission for claiming that Jesus is the only way of salvation, Mackay's *Global Warning* is timely. With good research and careful reasoning Mackay presents us with the informed vision which fired the conviction of the great men and women of God from Paul down to Hudson Taylor. It is a clarion call for us to wake up to the insidious influences of the pluralism and relativism of this new millennium.

Rev. David Ellis,
Minister at Large,
OMF International

Here is a clear and incisive analysis of several obstacles facing today's church as we seek to fulfil our Lord's Great Commission. *Global Warning* is a soul-stirring wake up call for Christians living in a self-absorbed age. It will rekindle your heart with a passion for world evangelisation.

Dr. John F. MacArthur
Grace Community Church,
California

Mission is the *raison-d'être* of the Christian Church. Yet Christians can easily find a thousand different reasons for avoiding it. This book is an uncompromising critique of such evasiveness and should disturb every evangelical conscience. It should also fire us all to go and tell every man and woman, 'I have good news for you.'

Donald Macleod,
Free Church of Scotland College, Edinburgh

Jesus told his disciples to make disciples of all nations. This mission has been hampered in the past 150 years by two forces: theological liberalism, which denies the authority of Scripture and pluralism which denies the uniqueness of Christ. Take away the authority of Scripture and the uniqueness of Christ and Christianity ceases to exist. This book is a timely warning to all of us of the dangers of compromising the essential nature of the Christian faith, and is an urgent call to refocus on the Great Commission.

Dr. Andrew McGowan
Highland Theological College,
Dingwall, Scotland.

In these days of compromise and confusion when unexpectedly even in some honoured evangelical circles the clarity and compulsion of the Great Commission is being eroded, we have here a clear biblical apologetic for the words of Jesus, 'No-one comes to the Father except through me.' Man can come to God in no other way than through Jesus Christ. To this solid biblical premise Norman Mackay is committed. His book is a necessary analysis and a timely warning to today's world. It needs to be digested and applied.

Dr. Colin N. Peckham,
Faith Mission Bible College,
Edinburgh

This unique cutting-edge missions book will not be easy for some of us to digest, but the message is greatly needed at this moment in history.

George Verwer,
International Director,
Operation Mobilisation.

Global Warning

Global Warning

*Third Millennium Threats to Jesus'
Great Commission Mandate*

Norman Mackay

Christian Focus

© Norman Mackay
ISBN 1 85792 659 5
Published in 2001
by Christian Focus Publications, Geanies House, Fearn,
Ross-shire, IV20 1TW, Great Britain.

Cover design by Owen Daily

Printed and bound in Great Britain by
The Guernsey Press Co. Ltd., Guernsey, Channel Islands

Contents

Introduction: Chat Shows and the Great Commission Mandate 9

PART ONE: Spiritual War on a Global Scale

1. A Nation Self-destructing: a prophetic lament 15

2. Global Spiritual Advance: a present reality 19

3. The Design And Goal Of History: a biblical vision 23

4. Becoming a World Christian: the principle of alignment 27

PART TWO: The Great Deception

Introduction: Selling a False Sense of Security 41

5. Religious Pluralism 43

6. Ecumenism: Evangelicals and Catholics together 59

7. Wideness in God's Mercy 67

8. Eternal Punishment: a conspiracy of silence 95

9. Consequences of Deception 103

PART THREE: Seize The Day

10. Symptoms of Decay: the real issue 109

11. Striking Back 113

CONCLUSION: Asking the Right Questions 157

Bibliography 163

References 167

At the heart of the teaching of the New Testament lie a few fundamental burning concerns. The chief of these is a desire for the glory of God. The means by which that is to be promoted is the evangelisation of the world.

Professor Sinclair Ferguson,
Add To Your Faith

Introduction

Chat Shows and the Great Commission Mandate

Chat shows are big business. Every day worldwide audiences switch on to savour personal stories and discussion topics which are increasingly bizarre. Breaking the boundaries is necessary in order to secure ratings. Breaking boundaries also has a subliminal effect upon us. It gradually legitimises that which was previously unacceptable.

> 'and it came to pass that as though it had been a *trivial thing* for him to walk in the sins of Jeroboam that he took as his wife Jezebel...and he went and served Baal and worshipped him' (1 Kings 16:31).

As the Church enters the first part of the third millennium, theological boundaries are being broken concerning the validity and urgency of the Great Commission mandate. This is no light thing. The unthinkable is becoming acceptable.

Prayer meetings for world mission have always held a special place in my heart. My wife and I were introduced at one such meeting. Our concern to be part of God's redemptive vision to reach the unreached peoples of our planet was conceived and nurtured during such prayer times. Moreover, most people we ever admired or held in high esteem were to be found regularly on their knees praying for missionaries, or indeed were themselves missionaries who shared about the great works of God in today's post-modern world. The missionaries were our spiritual 'heroes', especially the faith missionaries. They were not simply informed about God, but had actually been trained in the ways of God. Many of them had proven God in the furnace of life. Many could easily have written a powerful personal account of God's faithfulness to those who honour him.

Something else about these missionaries related to their sacrificial lifestyle. Living in a society defined primarily by material wealth, great numbers of missionaries had turned their back on a substantial income from secular employment to live on a survival-level monthly allowance.

The maps, overhead transparencies, facts and statistics all added to the thrill. Contrary to the widespread notion that there was a great falling away from the Christian faith, we discovered the gospel was actually spreading around the globe, and people groups all across the planet were coming to faith in Christ. Indeed if the end of the world was near, it was not because of some great apostasy, but rather because the remaining unreached peoples were near to being evangelised. Soon, we ourselves were caught up in God's wider plan for the nations. This consuming passion for the evangelisation of the world has been the main shaping factor in our lives for the past twenty years. We trust it will continue to be so for the remainder of our days.

Not everyone, though, shares the aspirations of the missionary. Indeed there is a growing hostility towards the notion that the peoples of the world can come to know God only through Christ. Doctrinal boundaries – once solidly in place – are now being broken. The uniqueness of Christ and the validity of the Great Commission mandate are under attack.

But what is this Great Commission mandate? All the texts of the Bible which bear upon the issue may be summarised very succinctly by the words of the Apostle Paul in the first chapter of Romans. Speaking of the gospel and testifying to God's calling upon his life he declares:

> 'through whom we have received grace and apostleship to bring about the obedience of faith for the sake of his name among all the nations, including yourselves who are called to belong to Jesus Christ' (Rom. 1:5-6).

That the nations should become obedient to the commands of the gospel for the glory of Jesus' name was the supreme passion point of the apostle's life and worldview. Today not everyone shares his aspirations. Contemporary society is fast rendering it politically incorrect to speak of the Great Commission mandate. From all quarters this command of Jesus is being undermined and attacked.

My short-lived fling with chess took place in Russia. Lots of people play chess there. Indeed in the years we lived among Russians great numbers of them played chess in the public parks throughout the summer months. On occasion, one could find a rather unusual game taking place. One man would be working his way round ten chess boards, simultaneously pitting his skills against a whole range of opponents. The outcome? Well, he would win all the games! He simply never lost! The reasons were obvious. Apart from the superior skills of the master chess player, the locals in the park had a range of moves which were all pretty predictable and very much the same. For all the huffing and puffing around on the board, there was not much activity that was either original or convincing. The master chess player had seen it all before, and was well equipped to address such moves.

Contemporary literature, within which are contained exhortations to 'rethink' the need for the Great Commission and the evangelisation of those within other religions, is just like this: lots of moves, very predictable, but all much the same. God has anticipated such moves and – like the master chess player – has provided the perfect blueprint for addressing them. It is with a view to exposing these moves that this book has been written.

Perhaps, though, you have no time to read this book. You have picked it up and are wondering if there is one simple rule by which to evaluate the myriad of claims presently circulating about the continuing relevance of the Great Commission. That rule is this: *if the view being put forward weakens, detracts from or undermines the urgency of bringing the gospel to all peoples then it is not of God, but is a lie of the devil.*

PART ONE

Spiritual War on a Global Scale

war armed hostilities ... conflict. **art of war** strategy and tactics. **war of nerves** an attempt to wear down an opponent by psychological means. **war of attrition** a war in which each side seeks to wear out the other over a long period of time (*The Concise Oxford Dictionary,* 8th edition, Oxford University Press, Walton Street, Oxford, OX2 6DP).

CHAPTER ONE

A Nation Self-destructing: *a prophetic lament*

My wife and I travel. Not as much as some people. Nonetheless our travels have been significant enough, and our friendships international enough, to give us reasonable exposure to how God is working in the world as we enter the first stage of the third millennium. We are also British citizens. Returning home from overseas recently we could not help but take note of how much of our conversation as Christians in the UK tends to focus upon the low moral condition of the nation, and the dreadful spiritual climate within the Church in particular. Both of those concerns are of course quite legitimate. Indeed it is difficult to imagine a Christian person being unconcerned about such issues. Patrick Johnstone in his missions handbook, *Operation World* no doubt reflects the views of most of us concerning Britain:

> Spiritual need is highlighted by the increasing violence in the cities, high divorce, suicide and illegitimacy rates, and drug abuse which is paralleled by a growing number of younger people who have no contact with or knowledge of Christianity.' He continues, 'Strident propaganda of the New Age and eastern mystical cults has eroded the Judeo-Christian heritage to the point that public opinion is no longer Christian.[1]

In similar vein David Alton reviews the shame of Britain's tragic abortion story from 1967–1997 in his book, *Life after Death*. Christians from all confessions would benefit from reading Alton's book for the chilling inside story of the United Kingdom's moral decline.

Yes, the United Kingdom is in moral dire straits, and as such would appear to be reaping the harvest of a culture of self-destruction presently being experienced by much of western society. As Christians concerned for our nation's spiritual welfare we cannot choose to be blind to this fact. It is no wonder, then, that our conversation is inexorably drawn to such concerns. Moreover at times it seems our prayers about them go unanswered. Habakkuk experienced a similar perplexity of spirit, and indeed expressed identical concerns about the moral and spiritual state of Israel in his day:

> How long O Lord must I call for help,
> but you do not listen?
> Or cry out to you, 'Violence!'
> but you do not save?
> Why do you make me look at injustice?
> Why do you tolerate wrong?
> Destruction and violence are before me;
> there is strife, and conflict abounds.
> Therefore the law is paralysed
> And justice never prevails.
> The wicked hem in the righteous,
> so that justice is perverted (Hab. 1:1-4).

From all that is known of Israel at this time Habakkuk's 'state of the nation' address was not wide of the mark. Surely God was not unmoved by the prophet's anguish over the moral and spiritual bankruptcy of society at large. The need for renewal within the nation was not in doubt.

Nonetheless God had his own response to the overwhelming burden which Habakkuk was carrying upon his shoulders. From a heavenly perspective the prophet's immediate need was not a deeper consciousness of the nation's apostasy but rather an enlarged awareness and fuller revelation of God's present and sovereign dealings amongst the nations. The Lord replies:

> Look among the nations!
> Observe!
> Be astonished! Wonder!
> Because I am doing something in your days,
> You would not believe if you were told.

Now here is a powerful antidote to the sense of being weighed down by local and national affairs. God is indeed painting his redemptive plan on a large and expansive canvas. The danger, though, is that we miss the big picture.

CHAPTER TWO

Global Spiritual Advance: *a present reality*

How is it possible? How can we miss something so awesome, and continue as if it simply did not exist? Incredible? Not really. It happens all the time. As we just saw, Habakkuk himself missed what God was doing.

Six weeks before our wedding we were delirious with joy. We had just had a real twenty five carat gold answer to prayer! Someone had sent a letter through the post with a cheque in it. Yes, that had happened many times before, but this time it was no regular missionary support gift. Enclosed was a cheque designated specifically for the purchase of a house! God had just provided what was to us an enormous sum of money. In a state of disbelief we purchased a lovely home with a wonderful and uninterrupted view from the rear. We opened the curtains each morning to enjoy the busy life of the local canal as the ducks, swans and little waterhens seemed to awaken in unison to greet the day.

After a while, however, the wonder and adventure of that view were dulled by a growing familiarity. Thereafter unless time was taken to pause and reflect upon the beauty of the trees, canal and wildlife the whole scene seemed nothing more than a distant backdrop to the hustle and bustle of life. How easy it would have been to allow familiarity to rob us of something which previously had been so captivating.

Perhaps for many Christians the wonder of the whole Great Commission enterprise has been lost. Something that ought to pulsate at the forefront of our highest thoughts lies dormant in the background. Perhaps a little imagination will bring this home to us in full force. Suppose that every single evangelical church within a ten mile radius of your local fellowship is actually a daughter church planted through your own outreach programme. Incredible? Yes! Hard to imagine? Of course! But let's go further and allow our eyes and mind to roam all over the globe: peoples, nations, countries, continents. For a brief moment the notion is entertained that every single evangelical church on planet earth, both small and great, has come into being as a result of an orchestrated outreach conducted by your little church. Incredulous? Dreamlike? Let's face it, we simply have no frame of reference by which to consider the potential of this actually happening.

Yet in Old Testament times a little localised 'church' named Israel was the recipient of God's promises to this effect. According to the Old Testament promises there would come a day when the true faith embraced by this little fellowship of people would spread over the face of the whole earth. But how could this be? Who could possibly have summoned enough faith to even consider the possibility of these prophetic utterances being fulfilled? How could they be fulfilled? After all, a small house church led by one pastor (Isa. 51:2) seems an unlikely beginning for a universal plan of redemption. Yet we, today, are seeing this come to pass before our very eyes. Ours is the generation privileged to witness the fulfilment of promises which in the days of Abraham must have seemed so awesome and incredible as to beggar belief. Sadly, though, it seems that great numbers of us have lost the wonder of it all.

If there is one incontrovertible fact at this point in church history it is this: God is building his Church on a global scale with vast spiritual kingdoms and strongholds being won for Christ.

Worldshare, formerly known as *Christian Nationals,* is just one of a great number of missionary organisations from around the world. *Worldshare*'s present commitments involve the provision of fellowship, prayer and financial support from the Church in the West to around seventy partner ministries working in around fifty countries. They write,

> In a recent twelve month period our partner ministries: planted 580 churches (one every 15 hours); brought 59,000 people to Christ (one every 9 minutes); trained over 17,000 Christian people for service; gave practical assistance to 105,000 needy people.[2]

These astonishing figures are by no means unusual in today's world.

Surely the commission to Habakkuk to 'look' amongst the nations and 'observe', is once again a pertinent exhortation to all of us within the evangelical Church. For all too many of us it is terribly tempting to remain preoccupied with a narrow range of local and pastoral concerns. These concerns, though legitimate, weigh us down, and all too often leave us with little time or energy to engage in positive and constructive reflection. Yet it is this very 'looking' and 'observing' that God is eager to introduce Habakkuk to, and this at a time in history when the prophet had a multitude of national concerns on his mind.

It is important to take note of what God is *not* actually saying. God is not simply suggesting that familiarising himself with a broader picture will provide Habakkuk with a healthy escapism from the tedious demands of local affairs. Not at all. What God is saying is that furnishing ourselves with a clear-sighted awareness of the Kingdom of God's wider expansion has the power to uplift and engage our hearts, regardless of the weightiness of local concerns. In other words there is great comfort and value in considering our local battles within the context of the bigger war. Local battles may be fought and sometimes lost; but the war is certainly being won.

Patrick Johnstone writes, 'We are living in the time of the largest ingathering of people into the kingdom of God that the world has ever seen ... there has been a multiplication of Protestant missionary sending and support agencies over the past two centuries; this has become a world-wide phenomenon of great significance'.[3]

This perspective echoes the thoughts of Timothy Alford who in his foreword to John Brand's excellent book, *Learning about Mission*, writes:

> Among Christians in today's world there is something of an explosion of interest in the imperative mission of the Church. It is not yet of seismic proportions, but may become so.[4]

But should any of us really have doubted that this would one day be the case? Is this unprecedented spread of the gospel simply an unexpected turn of events? Surely not. Isaiah prophesies:

> For as the soil makes the young plant to come up,
> and a garden causes seeds to grow,
> so the Sovereign Lord will make righteousness and praise spring up before all nations (Isa. 61:11).

That these very things are happening right before our eyes cannot be doubted.

Who would have predicted only twenty five years ago that today 'praise' would be 'springing up' across the Central Asian states of the former Soviet Union? Who would have imagined that Mongolia would have a dynamic worshipping community; or that the Lord would be thrusting forth Korean and Brazilian missionaries into the harvest fields of the world? What expectancy could we have had of thrilling Church growth in Indonesia? And what of the wonderful Bible translation progress that has been made? All of this is quite unprecedented in the history of the Church, and continues to gather momentum! The story just goes on and on!

As statisticians such as Johnstone and Barrett indicate, we are not speaking here about some abstract or theoretical position. All of the above development in world mission is quite simply an empirically verifiable reality. Look among the nations! Observe! Be astonished! Wonder!

Now the staggering implication of what has gone before is this: the evangelisation of the world, in terms of peoples, nations, tribes and tongues, is a realisable task in this, our generation. No longer need we speak in generalities about the 'masses', the 'lost' or 'a world without Christ'. Rather we are speaking of measurable and realisable evangelistic goals which, when accomplished, would enable us to state that most people groups on the planet have been witnessed to or reached with the gospel to a greater or lesser extent. With strenuous effort and commitment from the evangelical Church over the next twenty five years we could in this generation witness that which Habakkuk could only foresee:

> For the earth will be filled with the knowledge of the Lord;
> As the waters cover the sea (Hab. 2:14).

CHAPTER THREE

The Design And Goal Of History: *a biblical vision*

Central to the history of redemption is a more general philosophy of history. According to the Scriptures history under the sovereign control of almighty God is not only moving inexorably towards a predetermined end, but presses even the worst acts of sinful man into its service. God uses the ruthless Babylonians, for example, for his purposes:

> I am raising up the Babylonians, that ruthless and impetuous people, who sweep across the whole earth to seize dwelling-places not their own. They are a feared and dreaded people; they are a law unto themselves and promote their own honour (Hab. 1:6-7).

Now is not this a life-shaping truth? Even the very foreign policies and powerful expansionist aspirations of governments or military dictatorships are swallowed up in the interests of God's plan of redemption.

Repeatedly we see the reality of this powerful truth being outworked in the arena of everyday life. Understandably the workings of God in this regard are easier to see retrospectively. We are, for example, all by now very familiar with the ordering of political and cultural events under the rule of the Roman empire. On the one hand this corrupt empire functioned as a progressively evil and anti-Christian super-state. In the moral realm society was sinking about as low as it could go. Yet simultaneously the very *pax Romana* created by this superpower conveyed enormous strategic advantages for the spread of the gospel. Consider the following factors:

Political Factors
The Roman authorities, despotic though they were, nonetheless enforced a military peace throughout the empire. As a result safe travel was a distinct possibility.

Economic Factors
Additionally, the commercial and trade needs of the empire required a huge infrastructure. Well engineered and highly maintained roads allowed for rapid and effective travel.

Linguistic Factors
Given the range and diversity of people groups within the empire the facility of the Greek language as a common medium allowed for general and effective communication.

The point is this: God's plan of redemption does not progress by skipping around the periphery of international politics. Rather, God, in the exercise of his sovereignty, raises up and casts down nations and political states in accordance with the exercise of his world-wide plan of redemption.

Perhaps no modern day situation offers such a striking analogy of the rise and fall of the Roman empire as the cataclysmic events surrounding the emergence and collapse of the former Soviet Union.

Few westerners can ever really appreciate the enormity of the physical, spiritual and emotional suffering that the Russian and other peoples of the former USSR have experienced. Even now for many ordinary people the promised freedoms of capitalism have resulted in nothing more than humiliating poverty, a loss of dignity and the overt practice of brutal and organised crime.

Yet the fact is that in future days church historians will surely recount that the very claustrophobia and oppressiveness of the communist state with all its accompanying evils actually served the redemptive purposes of God. Indeed these very forces that robbed people of their individual value and dignity only served to heighten a longing to engage with the ultimate questions of life. From St. Petersburg to the Caucasus, down through Central Asia and on up to Siberia great numbers of people have come to faith in Christ. Just thirty years ago this would have seemed quite unthinkable.

It is not simply that God is making the most of his opportunities, or the best of a bad situation. But rather the bad situations are being used to further the cause of Christ in his world, and his plan of redemption.

This 'shaking of the nations' is not without purpose. Indeed this anticipated universal expansion and transformational impact of the Messiah's kingdom on the earth is perhaps the most thrilling of Old Testament prophetic themes.

> He will rule from sea to sea, and from the river to the ends of the earth. The desert tribes will bow before him and will lick the dust.
> The Kings of Tarnish and of distant shores will bring tribute to him: the kings of Sheba and Seba will present him gifts.
> All kings will bow down to him and all nations will serve him (Ps. 72:8-11).

Commenting upon such powerfully prophetic words long before there was little evidence to indicate their fulfilment William Jay (1769-1853), a nonconformist leader, had written:

> We also rejoice in hope. We have many and express assurances in the Scriptures which cannot be broken, of the universal spread and reign of Christianity which are not yet accomplished. Nothing has yet taken place in the history of Divine grace wide enough in extent, durable enough in continuance, powerful enough in energy, blessed enough in enjoyment, magnificent enough in glory, to do anything like justice to these predictions and promises. Better days therefore are before us notwithstanding the forebodings of many.

This progressive and dynamic expansion of Christ's Kingdom is further affirmed by means of three parables found in Matthew 13. The parables of the wheat field, the mustard seed and the leaven all speak of a gradual and inexorable expansion of the Kingdom, both qualitatively and quantitatively.

Nonetheless, boxed in as we are to our present experience of space-time history, many of us simply fail to grasp the colossal extent to which the Kingdom of God has actually expanded throughout the last two hundred and fifty years alone. The truth-value of these powerful parables is not lying dormant until some future event makes them relevant to a new generation. On the contrary, these parables are quite simply a stunning commentary on the de-facto world situation today. A cursory glance at the contemporary world from a Kingdom perspective confronts us powerfully with the present day outworking of the truth of Christ's Kingdom parables.

This design, therefore, and its accompanying momentum of past, future and contemporary events is moving towards a predetermined end. The goal of history culminates thus:

> After this I looked and there was before me a great multitude that no one could count, from every nation, tribe, people and language standing before the throne and in front of the Lamb. They were wearing white robes and were holding palm branches in their hands. And they cried out in a loud voice:
>
> Salvation belongs to our God,
> who sits on the throne, and to the Lamb (Rev. 7:9).

CHAPTER FOUR

Becoming a World Christian:
the principle of alignment

That the Kingdom of God is advancing, and that history is a running commentary on this, should not be in doubt. The main question for many of us, though, as we witness the twenty first century advance of the gospel amongst the Gypsy, Mongolian, Russian, Central Asian, Korean and other peoples of the world is this: are we actively and innovatively aligning ourselves with the present global spread of the gospel message? Put another way: does the Church's God-given responsibility for the evangelisation of our global village impact our lives in a radical, or even meaningful, way?

It is said of King David,

> After he had served the purpose of God in his own generation he fell asleep and was laid among his fathers, and underwent decay (Acts 13:36).

According to this passage one of the striking features of David's life was that he sought to actively and creatively align himself with the purposes of God as revealed to his generation. The disturbing thing about many of us as professing evangelicals is that if our lifestyles reflect our priorities, then sadly many of us remain coldly indifferent to God's wider purposes.

It is bemusing to note the great number of evangelical Christians, including ministers and pastors, who make little attempt to aspire, as David did, to align themselves with God's broader purposes for this generation. Enlarging our awareness to engage zealously in cross-cultural and trans-national missionary outreach simply does not happen for many of us. To be sure as we have already noted there is an unprecedented spreading of the good news in this generation. It is all too clear, though, that this continues to be carried out primarily by a small minority within the Church.

It could also be suggested, at the risk of seeming slightly uncharitable, that much of our praying for world mission is somewhat short-sighted. In what way? Consider, for example, our praying for Muslims in the Middle East, North Africa and Central Asia. Or better still, the unreached of India and Pakistan. How often have we prayed along the following lines, 'Lord, grant open doors to spread the Word to the people of Pakistan!' or, 'Lord, do not withhold visas!' Yet as we pray those very prayers, within two hundred yards of our church buildings live huge Pakistani and Indian communities, all but unreached with the gospel.

In the UK today the Church has a wonderful harvest on its very doorstep. To reap that harvest no visas are required, open doors lie before us and a common language is mostly in place. Herein lies our opportunity to evidence the sincerity of our prayers, and to act on them in real people's lives.

The same could also be suggested in respect of financial giving. How often do we pray for the Lord to provide, or to open the windows of heaven, for some much needed overseas project. The reality has to be faced that meanwhile many of us could simply withdraw a small proportion of our income from the local cashline machine to meet that need, and hardly miss it at all! Yet contributing to the advance of world mission is sometimes perceived by us as evangelicals not as a fundamental biblical responsibility, and indeed a privilege, but as giving a 'handout' or 'donation' to a good cause. For many, sadly, this reflects the relative unimportance we attach to the ultimate goal of Christ's death, namely the salvation and redemption of his universal Church. How sad when finance for local church building improvements are almost invariably viewed as having a priority claim over Christ's missionary cause. Touching upon this issue in an altogether different context Professor Donald Macleod of the Free Church of Scotland writes,

> Under present conditions, unfortunately a huge proportion of church income goes towards the maintenance of buildings ... In the New

Testament money and deacons were primarily for the poor (*Scottish Bulletin of Evangelical Theology*)

Yet this centrifugalism which so characterises great numbers of our local church fellowships is simply not part of the New Testament worldview. The frequently injected dichotomy between 'local responsibilities' and 'overseas concerns' encourages a church to prioritise in favour of one against the other, and introduces a distinction unknown in New Testament times. All New Testament Christians were expected to see their place in the bigger picture. Jesus said:

> But you will receive power when the Holy Spirit comes upon you and you will be my witnesses in Jerusalem, and in all Judea and Samaria, and to the ends of the earth (Acts 1:8).

The assumption here is that we will all be aligning ourselves with this dynamic and outward movement to the peoples of the world. The idea of 'limited identification' or 'Jerusalem only' involvement is simply not envisaged as an available option. Local church leaders who perceive the global concerns of Christ as an optional extra have, sadly, missed the central thrust of our biblical commission.

The Key To The Missionary Problem by Andrew Murray sums up the situation well,

> It is one thing for a minister to be an advocate and supporter of missions: it is another and very different thing for him to understand that missions are the chief end of the church, and therefore the chief end for which his congregation exists. It is only when this truth masters him in its spiritual power that he will be able to give the subject of missions its true place within his ministry.[5]

Becoming a world-Christian thus begins with a recognition that God's redemptive concern extends well beyond our local and limited aspirations. It is furthered by the acceptance that his aspirations for us at a local level involve the widening of our horizons. In many cases this can in fact be done without ever travelling outside our own country. In many major cities of the world we find people from a huge percentage of the world's nations. The UK, as indicated earlier, has also very rapidly become a multi-ethnic society. For many of us, then, the question is not really, 'To go, or not to go?' but rather, 'To get involved or to remain unconcerned?'

Any one of the following ministries, for example, could be taken up immediately by most local churches. There are, of course, many more opportunities for mission involvement, but the following represent ways of engaging in world evangelism that require only a little time and effort.

i) *Gospel broadsheets*

Across the United Kingdom many Christians have pioneered international cross-cultural evangelism on a global scale without ever leaving the country! The concept of gospel broadsheets has been well known within evangelical missionary circles for years. The idea is quite simple. Recognising, for example, English as a major language in the world of international communications, advertisements for one-page English-language news-sheets are placed within newspapers in a country where English is widely known and desirable as a second language. By simply filling in the coupon and returning it to a UK address the person receives, free of charge, an A4 gospel broadsheet within which testimonies and biblical truths are presented in easy-read English. Such broadsheets are simply the format for disseminating the seed of the Word of God, and are thoroughly enjoyed and appreciated by thousands of people.

In doing this, we can be optimistic about the results. Isaiah 55:10, 11 reminds us,

> For as the rain and snow come down from heaven,
> And do not return there without watering the earth,
> And making it bear and sprout,
> And furnishing seed to the sower and bread to the eater:
> So shall my word which goes forth from my mouth:
> It shall not return to me empty,
> Without accomplishing what I desire,
> And without succeeding in the matter for which I sent it.

As the gospel broadsheets are posted off by volunteer dispatch teams, others are ready to take up correspondence with those who upon reading the broadsheets write off with questions concerning the material they are reading.

Thus it is quite possible to involve oneself in international evangelism and to do so in a very meaningful and innovative way – without ever leaving home!

In the wonderful little book, *Access without Visa* which documents the story of the SOON broadsheet ministry we read the testimony of one elderly lady who in advancing years still wished to be part of the world-wide missionary movement:

> Phyllis Knottley believed God was calling her to a new ministry but at 69 she wondered what she could do ... It was Wednesday before she had a chance to see the missionary exhibition. Looking at the stands her attention was drawn to the name SOON! Although aware of the ministry she had dismissed it, thinking that it simply involved addressing envelopes. That evening however her eyes focused on a single panel marked 'Answering Problem Letters'. Suddenly everything clicked into place: writing, counselling, sharing her Bible knowledge and practical experience. She could do all of them without having to leave her chair![6]

Presently, over 1,000 UK dispatch teams mail 750,000 easy-English broadsheets every three months to well over 100 countries around the world. Every week letters of inquiry pour in from such far away places as Mongolia and China. Pen friends are established and follow-up letters are written by dedicated volunteers who are only too happy to be part of what God is doing through ordinary people caught up with His vision for worldwide evangelisation.

Over the years many have come to Christ from all around the world through this proven ministry. The cost? A stamped envelope and a few nights per month writing letters or addressing envelopes.

ii) *The Internet*
In the days of the apostles it was the Roman roads that helped in the logistics of spreading the faith. Today we have the electronic pathway.

21st century technology serves as a catalyst for futuristic thinking. Church history testifies to God's vision to involve 'innovators' whose imagination and creativity are powerful spiritual tools. The internet and its exploitation by Great Commission thinkers is opening up a 'super-highway of holiness' for the gospel. The internet can be a radical and powerful means for sending the good news of Christ around the nations at lightning speed. All of us with PCs and modems can interface with the uttermost parts of the globe.

Recently I found myself in a shop that happened to be owned by a Muslim family from Pakistan. They were in fact very zealous and missionary-minded Muslims, and almost immediately upon hearing that I was a follower of Jesus began to speak openly about Islam. I have found in sharing with Muslim men that it is usually a pretty futile exercise to engage in debate in the presence of an audience. Almost inevitably the discussion generates into heated argument. Yet here were Muslim men who seemed to want to talk about God, yet not betray their questionings to those around.

How could these discussions be followed up without a threat element? Suddenly it seemed obvious. In all probability they had PCs at home. Sharing the gospel with Muslims by e-mail became a reality. It is a more or less private and personal means of communication, and allows time to formulate considered replies. Light without heat!

Information technology and the phenomenon of the personal computer are opening up fresh horizons for us as world-Christians. By means of the personal computer and electronic mail it is possible for millions of people to be communicating with each other from all around the globe! Thus the dissemination of salt, light and spiritual truth by means of computer technology is a present potential just beginning to be fulfilled.

Great Commission web-sites provide immediate opportunity to proclaim the gospel in areas of the world which would otherwise remain untouched, apart from the witness of a few dedicated local believers, and perhaps a small number of tentmaking missionaries. By simply purchasing any one of a number of books written for Christians a church can be introduced by the internet to a whole new world of international and cross cultural communication. Experienced people are available to help us effectively communicate the good news of Jesus using this amazing medium.

Now would it not be an exciting thing if the purchase and setting up of internet facilities within the church for the purposes of international outreach became a hot issue for the next church business meeting... It cannot be stressed enough just how important it is that as Christian churches we see the potential in harnessing technological innovation, and pressing such into the service of the Church.

An example of this futuristic thinking can be seen in the work and ministry of the Highland Theological College situated in Dingwall, Scotland. The College exists to provide opportunities for men and women to study the Christian faith on a full-time or part-time basis. Of particular significance here, though, is that the college is presently engaged in the exploration of theological education by means of video-conferencing. Keeping in step with such new media is essential if as Great Commission Christians we wish to make the most of all opportunities to spread the word of truth.

As is revealed in Hebrews chapter 11, God loves to talk about the faith of his children. God seems to take great delight in our being creative, innovative and futuristic in our thinking when it comes to spreading His Word.

iii) *Strategic Sponsorship*
Another category of strategic and powerful involvement in world evangelisation is quite simply that of sponsorship. Making money go a long way is an essential part of stewardship, and a very great deal can be accomplished by 'Great-Commission giving' on the part of those who have been blessed with even an average income within the western world. It is often possible to sponsor a local evangelist in, for example, India, or to finance a young missionary candidate through a local Bible College for a minimal sum of money.

For many years my wife and I were closely associated with faith missions whose members (including ourselves) took the view that one should never appeal for finance. Behind this principled stance was a very noble faith maxim, summed up so clearly by Hudson Taylor, 'God's work done in God's way will never lack God's provision'. In adopting this faith principle many missionary agencies avoided the stereotyped 'appeals' for finance which, we believed, would 'put people off', or at least make them feel uncomfortable.

One down-side to this approach, though, is that it can by default conceal the fact that huge and strategic advances are often held up simply due to a lack of sponsorship. And as far as the Great Commission is concerned, money is not a necessary evil, but rather potential funding to be released strategically and prayerfully into the Lord's work.

Christians are called upon to be channels of blessing and the Scriptures employ a whole range of descriptive words to help us cultivate a proper attitude to our finances.

1. Giving with the heart
Such flows from compassion (2 Cor. 8:8), is responsive to need (Acts 11:28-30) and ought to be cheerfully done (2 Cor. 9:7).

2. Giving with the head
Such giving is systematic (1 Cor. 16:1-2), proportionate (1 Cor 16:2), principled (2 Cor. 9:6-7) and is sacrificial (Mark 12:43-44).

Now in the light of the above can any one of us really think of a single, genuine reason as to why we should not sponsor a little child for £10 a month to save her from a destitute existence on a Latin American rubbish heap? For just £10 a month a small child can receive all he or she needs to be clothed, fed, to attend a school (sometimes Christian) and at the same time participate in a local Bible club. It is heartbreaking when we hear of more being spent on pet food than on saving the lives of destitute children.

Given the colossal amount of finance we western evangelicals spend on ourselves, not to mention our state-of-the-art sound systems and church buildings, could it just be possible that we need to be a little less self- and entertainment- focused, and a little more zealous in releasing our resources on behalf of others.

Can we not view the strategic investment of finance in Great Commission ministry in a much more dynamic way? Through the strategic investment of capital, life-saving ministries can be released into peoples lives. As far as God is concerned, there is absolutely nothing unclean about finance in itself. It should be talked about openly, used wisely and seen as a powerful tool for the advance of the gospel around the globe.

By releasing finance into the Kingdom the impact of the church worldwide can surely be increased exponentially.

iv) *International travel*

International travel can be a wonderfully enriching experience. Indeed, great numbers of pastors and church members who make it a priority to travel every so often to visit overseas missionary locations testify to an enlarged vision and increased scope for ministry. This can be done by a church simply investing in, for example, a two or three week visit to a shanty town in Latin America, or a Bible college in India. Opportunities simply abound.

Such cross-cultural and transnational exposure has the potential to explode the tunnel vision which enslaves so many of our local fellowships, and at the same time serves as an opportunity to introduce the local church to the adventure of being part of something far greater and more exciting than we ever imagined.

Let's consider this another way. It is quite possible to read this book, agree with the general content, yet remain unmoved in spirit. On the other hand it is unlikely that after visiting, for example, a refuge centre in South East Asia for child prostitutes we could remain unconcerned. One overseas visit can be a major pivotal event in the life and ministry of a pastor. As Rev. John Brand, U.K. Director of Africa Inland Mission testifies,

> As the Pastor of a small inner city church in London I was keen to have a personal involvement in world mission that would also be of benefit to my church. I had begun a missions programme in the church and we regularly had speakers from various agencies visiting us, broadening our vision of what God was doing in the world.
>
> I then received an invitation from Africa Inland Mission to join

their UK Council and gladly accepted. Here I had the opportunity to be directly involved in the work of a large international and interdenominational mission agency and I relished it. The Council is responsible for directing the work of the UK Office of AIM International and its members serving overseas. When I moved from my London church to another charge in Liverpool, my new church were keen for me to keep my commitment to AIM, recognising that there would be benefit in it for them as well. As well as my attendance at Council meetings in London, I had missionaries visiting our home, was involved in the screening and interviewing of candidates and spoke at AIM and other missionary conferences. In addition to my AIM activities I was chairing a national group whose burden was to get local churches committed to world mission and generally my active commitment to world mission became greater and greater so that there came a point in time when I really had to decide whether the Lord was calling me to be a pastor with a world mission commitment or be fully involved in mission.

Around that time I accepted an invitation to go to Madagascar, one of AIM's fields of service, to lead a Preachers' Conference and see for myself the work being done there. While this was in the planning stage, AIM's Scottish Secretary resigned and I began to think that God was leading me to take over that role. After much prayer and consultation my wife and I were convinced that this was indeed what God was saying and so I resigned from the church. In the Lord's timing, my trip to Madagascar came just a month before my leaving Liverpool but provided the confirmation, if confirmation I needed, of the Lord's leading.

Now, as Director of AIM in Europe, I am totally convinced that for the local church to play its full and rightful role in the working out of the Great Commission, the church leadership must be convinced and committed. There is no better way of achieving that than for the pastor to have a personal involvement in mission and while, in most cases, it will not lead down the same route that God has led me, it will undoubtedly lead to great blessing for minister, church and world mission alike.[7]

Thus a simple choice to invest time and energy in short visits enables God to internationalise our worldview and broaden our horizons.

To leave these concerns to the odd individual who has an

'interest in missions', or who feels 'called to go' is really to miss the mark altogether. Postage stamps, envelopes, e-mail, brief overseas visits and a small sum of money – hardly the stuff of immense sacrifice. Indeed, as the world gravitates towards a global village experience many of our churches are very quickly running out of excuses as to why we are not broadening our philosophy of ministry to incorporate reaching the remaining unreached peoples of the world.

PART TWO

The Great Deception

deceit. 1. the act or process of deceiving or misleading, esp, by concealing the truth. 2. a dishonest trick or stratagem. 3. willingness to deceive (*The Concise Oxford Dictionary,* 8th edition, Oxford University Press).

Introduction

Selling a False Sense of Security

Despite the wonderful opportunities available to many of us to be part of what God is doing in the world, there may well be other forces at work which threaten to anaesthetise the Church. And note the timing – this, just as the push is on to evangelise the world's remaining unreached peoples.

Given the triumphant, expansive and fairly rampant advance of the Kingdom of God throughout the last 250 years, it is not surprising to find that this final push for the evangelisation of the world is drawing focused satanic opposition. This is indeed the case. Sadly, though characteristically, although that which threatens to undermine all that God is doing arose from outside the evangelical church, it is also being embraced within. As we engage with the new millennium a spirit of error is abroad which threatens the very *raison-d'être* of the world missionary movement. This spirit of error is manifest in various strands of teaching which, if taken together and drawn to a logical conclusion, would lead us to believe that the evangelisation of the remaining unreached peoples of the world is at best a waste of time, and at worst a rather arrogant presumption.

Undeniably, one of the hallmarks of Satan's work is that of enticing undiscerning Christians to believe something which ought not in the first instance even to be considered. The areas of thought outlined in the following chapters combine into a formidable contemporary assault on the Great Commission of the Lord Jesus Christ.

CHAPTER FIVE

Religious Pluralism

Religious pluralism incorporates a variety of viewpoints which are nonetheless held together by a few core common denominators. The underlying assertion throughout the movement is that all the great world religions can provide a pathway to God, and that all the sacred books such as the Koran and the Bible contain revealed and saving truth from God. At the most basic level the controlling assertion is that all religious experience involves an encounter with the same transcendent Being (God). Despite its differing expressions, it is said, this experience can be a saving experience. The actual truth or falsity of any claim relating to a religious experience is not to be assessed by virtue of its informational content, but rather by whether or not it leads to a more harmonious relationship to the world around us. Thus all propositions made by different religious faiths are subordinated to the religious experience itself. The experience is the key issue, since God (the transcendent Being) is beyond our comprehension.

In this grand scheme biblical Christianity is viewed as one emerging pattern within a kaleidoscope of religious and redemptive possibilities. We may, it is thought, find some redemptive truth within the Christian worldview, but this cannot exclude saving revelation within other world religions.

At a foundational level the issue here is clearly one of authority. At the very outset this viewpoint entails a wholesale rejection of Christ as the unique and exclusive revelation of God, accompanied by a corresponding denial of the uniqueness of the gospel message.

However ours is not the first generation to flirt with such ideas. Though often touted as the ground-breaking fruits of 21st century reflection, this idea is not at all an original one. In the days of the Roman Empire such notions were commonplace. As Edward Gibbon has pointed out in his now monumental work, *The Decline and Fall of the Roman Empire,*

The Greek, the Roman, and the Barbarian, as they met before their respective altars easily persuaded themselves that under various names and with various ceremonies they adored the same deities.[8]

Now Gibbon's comments are singularly unfortunate for those who under the guise of contemporary scholarship would have us believe that some innovative and original thought is at work here. Indeed, what is perhaps even more revealing is that in Gibbon's estimation the intellectual climate within which this idea spawned was at best mediocre. Thus this 'melting pot' approach to religion was not so much the outcome of robust theological investigation, but rather was symptomatic of a lack of such.

To the assertion that saving truth is to be found in the gods of Rome the early Church had but one answer. Depicting the exile and martyrdom of Cyprian of North Africa in 258, Dr. Nick Needham records the details of conversations held between Cyprian and the then governor of North Africa. These conversations led to Cyprian's murder. Consider the following excerpts:

> *(The soldiers of the governor of North Africa, Paternus, bring Cyprian into his presence)*
> *Paternus:* The most sacred emperors, Valerian and Gallienus, have honoured me with letters requiring all who do not observe Rome's religion to profess their return to Roman rites of worship. I have therefore asked you by the name of what religion do you call yourself? What is your answer?
> *Cyprian:* I am a Christian and a bishop. I know of no other gods beside the one true God, who made heaven and earth, the sea, and everything in it. We Christians serve this God; we pray to him day and night for ourselves, for all mankind and for the health of the emperors themselves.
>
> *One Year later a new governor Galerius Maximus recalled Cyprian from exile*:
> *Galerius*: The most sacred emperors have commanded you to conform to the Roman rites of worship.
> *Cyprian:* I refuse.
> *Galerius:* Think about the consequences.

Cyprian: Do as you must. In so clear a case, I do not care about the consequences.
Galerius: ...The authority of the law shall be sealed in your blood. It is the sentence of this court that Thascius Cyprian be executed by the sword.
Cyprian: Thanks be to God!⁹

If religious pluralism was a valid option at the time, then certainly the early Church had no notion of it.

Neither, it seems, did the Korean Christians who suffered cruelly during the years of Japanese occupation. Any belief in religious pluralism would certainly have made life very much easier for the Korean Church. Esther Ahn Kim, who was imprisoned and tortured for her faith during that time, tells her remarkable story as to exactly what was expected of Christians during the occupation:

> The Japanese had built shrines in all the villages of our captive land forcing our people to place miniature shrines in every school, government office and household. Then had come the latest blasphemy. Shrines were placed in every Christian church and police were dispatched to every service to see that every person who came in bowed to the pagan god before the worship service.[10]

She recalls:

> Anyone who refused to bend his knee in the Japanese shrines – whether missionary, pastor, or deacon – was mercilessly tortured once he was found out. His fate was that of a traitor.[11]

The first day of the month was the day appointed by the Japanese as the time when Esther Ahn Kim and her fellow teachers and pupils from the Christian school where she taught were expected to engage in a mass pilgrimage to the shrine of the sun-goddess. She continues:

> 'Attention!' A strident order shrilled above the murmuring of the crowd. The people straightened, line by line. We were accustomed to being subservient for we had been captives of the Japanese for

more than thirty seven years. 'Our profoundest bow to Amaterasu Omikamai (the sun-goddess)!'

As one person that enormous crowd followed the shouted order by bending the upper half of their bodies solemnly and deeply. Of all the people at the shrine I was the only one who remained erect, looking straight at the sky.[12]

This course of action served as a catalyst for one of the most moving testimonies in modern church history.

Throughout the history of the church religious pluralism has never been something God's Holy Spirit has honoured. This is the testimony of the Church world-wide.

Neither are the underlying philosophical assertions which accompany religious pluralism particularly original. Any undergraduate student of philosophy will soon discover old friends such as Kant metamorphosing in religious guise throughout 'contemporary' publications. Old problems are also evident. Consider the following examples.

(a) *The Rejection of the Principle of Non Contradiction*
Central to religious pluralism is the somewhat bizarre claim that contradictory and opposing truth claims can each be true! When Christianity asserts, for example, that there is only one way of salvation, and that there is no such thing as reincarnation, yet other world religions flatly contradict or deny this, there is no need to be perplexed. The answer is quite simply that these contradictions don't actually exist at all. Everyone, it seems, is right!

It does not take too much imagination to appreciate the joy that such a discovery would bring to millions of schoolchildren. No one need ever fail an exam again. All answers would be right! One child can suggest that the capital of France is Hong Kong, another can suggest London and a third Paris. Yet despite the conflicting nature of the answers all claims would be equally valid. They only *seem* contradictory.

On hearing this assertion most people would doubtless concede that the pluralistic argument is at best struggling from the very outset. In order, though, to avoid pushing the self-destruct button, religious pluralists have advanced various defensive arguments to prop up their claims. Unfortunately these arguments would appear to simply delay the pushing of the button, since they all suffer from the same internal contradictions. Let us consider just a few:

Firstly, one response suggests that while it is true that, for example, a banana cannot be both a banana and a plum at the same time, this way of thinking is only valid in certain dimensions of experience. The principle of non-contradiction applies to the foregoing example about bananas and plums but not, it is held, to the spiritual dimension of reality. The religious dimension, we are told, involves a kind of truth which transcends all of this self evident logic. Hence contradictions about who God is and what he has said are not a cause for concern. Once again the assertion is that we are not rejecting the principle of non-contradiction as such, but simply stating that it does not apply to the realm of religious knowledge.

Probably the first question that pops into the mind of any rational person on hearing this type of claim is simply: how is such knowledge about this non logical realm of reality come by? Indeed, how can such knowledge be possible? The problem here is that someone is claiming to have information about a non rational dimension of reality. But if this dimension is not subject to rational comprehension or laws of logic, by what means, then, has our information about it been attained, and how can that be communicated? If this information can indeed be understood and communicated, then it ceases to remain outwith the realms of rational understanding. If, however, the opposite is true then how can someone possibly be in receipt of this information which, it is stated, is beyond our grasp!

Secondly, a related problem is the question as to whether or not we are to regard this claim concerning the non-applicability of laws of logic as true. Given that any truth claim is of necessity predicated upon the law of non-contradiction, the statement concerning the existence of a realm of experience not subject to the laws of non-contradiction self-destructs. All affirmations or denials of a truth are predicated upon the law of non-contradiction.

The 'catch 22' here is quite simply that we are all subject to, and instinctively presuppose, laws of logic in our thinking. As we read this very sentence the act of distinguishing one word from another is evidence that we are employing the law of non-contradiction. As Christian philosopher Gordon Clark has stated many times:

> Logic is irreplaceable. To repeat – even if it seems wearisome: logic is fixed, universal, necessary and irreplaceable. As such its laws cannot be deduced from nor abstracted from experience.[13]

It should be obvious to all that society would be ill advised to take seriously a theory of religious knowledge that makes the taking leave of our senses a pre-condition for gaining spiritual information!

Other attempts have been made to avoid a rejection of the laws of logic while at the same time continuing to affirm the validity and truthfulness of contradictory religious claims. Such attempts involve a commitment to the notion that there is indeed only one supreme being, but our responses to and cognitive awareness of this being are conditioned by historical and cultural factors. These cultural differences provide an interpretative framework through which we conceive God, and our experience of him will be represented and expressed in keeping with this framework. Thus the great differences between world religions are simply culturally conditioned patterns within a religious kaleidoscope. Each religious expression has its own unique pattern yet, it is held, all are a valid expression of the one entity. No one is any less legitimate than another.

It is difficult, however, for someone who holds this view of cultural conditioning to proceed much further in his or her assertions. If one's religious worldview is culturally conditioned, then of necessity so is the viewpoint just being espoused. The problem is that someone is claiming to transcend cultural conditioning just long enough to reassure us that it is something we can never do.

A related problem naturally arises here as to whether or not we are in a position to verify which, if any, of these experiences do in fact provide an encounter with God? There must be some objective confirmation available to us beyond the experience itself which will enable us to test this claim. Without a 'truth-test' someone could equally suggest that these religious experiences are all false. Given that we have no objective truth-test, this claim cannot be invalidated or confirmed.

In short, one cannot escape the fact that in order to know something about the nature of God, we must first have some definitive truth concerning God, by which to evaluate the truth or falsity of claims about him. Without this the arguments cannot get off the starting blocks.

Thus the philosophical base of religious pluralism is one quite devoid of credibility. At the touch of a button the arguments which undergird these religious claims destroy themselves.

(b) *Religious Language – inadequate and misunderstood*
The 20th century was replete with theories of language. Philosophies of language have been pressed into service with a view to finding ways around the difficulties inherent within the acceptance of opposing religious truth claims. One common assertion to be found in much contemporary religious literature is that theological truth cannot be expressed in propositions, a proposition being simply the meaning conveyed by a sentence. This is a well worn theme in contemporary theology.

The idea of communicating theological truth by means of propositional statements is out of vogue. Human language, we are told, is insufficient to bridge the gap between man and God. Yet the Christian faith involves a belief in the fact that God has created man in his own image, and therefore informative, meaningful and rational communication between God and man is possible. The primary medium, therefore, by which God communicates is language.

A variation on this theme is the assertion that God is so 'wholly other' that he transcends all the human concepts we would use to establish his identity, or to say something about him.

At first glance the existence of a transcendent being of whom nothing can be predicated, and about whom nothing can be said, would appear to remove all problems in a world of religious diversity. It is not so much that everyone is equally correct (e.g. Muslims, Buddhists and Hindus) in what they say of God, but rather everyone is equally mistaken in the belief that such statements are indicative of any religious truth concerning God at all.

The first problem with this idea is this: how are we to know that it is in fact God we are encountering in the first place? If God is so wholly other, and I cannot in advance be forewarned as to what he is like, how am I to know that it is indeed this being I have encountered. What will enable me to distinguish a blinding encounter with God from a blinding encounter with a demon, or a UFO? Or, if you like, how may we distinguish a real experience of God from a false one?

The usual answer given to this type of question is far from impressive. Our experience of God, we are told, will be self-authenticating. God can be evoked, but not expressed, since he is incomprehensible. A religious encounter with God will, therefore, leave one aware that the experience was authentic, and as such it is a self-verifying experience. Once you've had it, you just know that it was an encounter with the wholly other transcendent being.

But *how* will we know this? How are we to verify to ourselves that it is God with whom we are in touch? Unfortunately, self-authentication will not do. It will not do, because no experience can be self-authenticating. We cannot appeal to the experience alone as support for the truth-claim associated with it. An experience is simply a condition, and as such is neither true nor false. It is simply an experience. As with the previous problems of cultural conditioning, some criteria objective to the experience are required to distinguish it from other experiences, and thus determine its truth or falsity. These, we are told, cannot be provided since the experience cannot even be described! But why cannot this experience be described? And if it cannot be described, we have to ask how someone knows that they have had it?

The second problem takes us back to the question – how it is possible to be in receipt of information which, we are assured, cannot be known? If God is wholly other, and as such incapable of being known, where did this information about his incomprehensibility come from? Surely the knowledge that God is incomprehensible is in itself knowledge about God? Similarly, if nothing about God can be communicated in propositions, then why should we be listening at all to religious pluralists talking about God!

Once all the pomp and ceremony have been stripped away from this talk about religious language, we are confronted with a whole range of claims which are at loggerheads with their own philosophical basis.

(c) *The Status of Religious Pluralistic Claims*

As should be clear by now, any idea of absolute and objective truth which excludes other truth-claims is anathema to the pluralistic conception of reality. However, once again we encounter self-destructive reasoning as pluralists seek to provide a basis for this position. The pluralistic view of reality which disallows the very possibility of objective, propositional and exclusive truth is itself a propositional, objective and exclusive truth-claim. Here we have a claim (for example, that there are many ways to God) which enjoys the status of a truth claim about religious knowledge, and as such disallows other claims which contradict it (such as, there is only one mediator between man and God).

At the level of epistemology, then, the striking credentials of religious pluralism as a system of thought would appear to be as follows: religious pluralism demands that its adherents accept something which they are at one and the same time obliged to reject, namely that one truth-claim is exclusively and objectively true. This means that the ultimate claim of religious pluralism – that there are many ways to God – self destructs as soon as it is conceived or expressed.

Despite the *reductio ad absurdum* character of religious pluralism, it remains true that such an illusory view of reality is being aggressively promoted as a politically correct perspective on world religion. Needless to say, within this approach to religion there is no logical or actual necessity for world-wide evangelisation, since we would only be preaching to the converted. Superfluous to say that within this school of thought little or no regard is paid to the actual claims or authority of the Bible. Neither is the Bible's own philosophy of religion taken as a starting point, or made reference to.

As is commonly acknowledged, the grass roots political expression of religious pluralism is represented by the inter-faith movement. Armed with the above pluralistic assertions the general dynamic of the movement is towards world-wide religious unity. Thus at the very core of this movement lurks a deep-seated hostility to the very notion of evangelical missionary activity.

It is, perhaps, all too easy to be dismissive of the inter-faith movement and religious pluralism. When a person insists that Buddhism, Hinduism and historical Christianity are really the same thing it is genuinely difficult to know what to say, or how to take such a view seriously. However leaving aside the more obvious philosophical difficulties two further points may be worthwhile noting. Both relate to a naivety which tends to characterise adherents of this idealistic movement:

(d) *Naivety concerning intolerance*
Generally speaking, societies dominated by other religious worldviews (e.g. Islam) do not ooze funds of goodwill towards Christianity. We mention Islam only because theoretically it, along with Judaism, ought to be the closest to the Christian worldview, claiming to be monotheistic and having, as we are told, great reverence for the Bible.

Contrary to what the inter-faith movement would like us to accept, other religions do not in fact see themselves as compatible with rival worldviews. Neither are the 'holy books' laced with common denominators in the way we are all encouraged to believe. The Koran, for example, denies, (i) the triune nature of God, (ii) the deity of Christ, (iii) the sonship of Christ, (iv) the crucifixion of Christ, and asserts a whole range of contrary teachings.

Attitudinally, Islam is not at all kindly disposed to those of other faiths. One Islamic magazine which regularly derides Christianity writes, quoting a recent book on the Bible,

> Whenever we read the obscene stories, the voluptuous debaucheries, the cruel and tortuous executions, the unrelenting vindictiveness, with which more than half the Bible is filled, it would be more consistent that we called it the word of a demon than the word of God.[14]

Now it would be a tall order even for the most enthusiastic of inter-faith adherents to extract a note of friendship from that statement.

Not that such hostility is restricted to Muslims. The *Evangelical Times* in its March, 1999 edition under the heading, 'Australian Missionary and Sons Die in India' writes as follows:

> An Australian evangelical missionary and his two sons have been killed by Hindu militants in Orissa, east India. Graham Staines (58), and sons Timothy (8) and Philip (10) were burned to death as they slept in their car following a prayer meeting at which Mr. Staines had preached. Mr. Staines had worked with leprosy patients for more than 30 years and was treasurer of the Evangelical Missionary Society of Mayurbhanj... The tragedy is the most serious incident in a year of violent attacks on Christians and missionaries in particular. Militant Hindu groups have declared themselves opposed to the presence of missionary societies in the country and have even begun advertising names and addresses in a development likely to incite further violence. There have been over 100 recorded attacks on Christians in the last two years and numerous church burning incidents.

Now these are not isolated statements or happenings. Hostility towards Christian people and their beliefs has been an integral part of international life throughout the twentieth century.

Not that Christians themselves have been exempt from expressing hostility towards others in society. Indeed, as Alister McGrath has pointed out in his excellent book, *Bridge Building*[15] one of the great difficulties in spreading the gospel in some parts of the world is the legacy of the unfortunate historical associations Christianity has in people's minds and experience. Societies which by and large have laid claim to a Christian cultural heritage have often seemed all too willing to Christianise racism, anti-semitism and much more.

Nonetheless the fact remains that the inter-faith movement would appear to have a perspective on world religion which simply cannot be reconciled with the everyday experience of minorities seeking to survive in a society dominated by majority religious worldviews.

(e) *Naivety regarding the demonic in other religions*
For many years Christian missionaries and national pastors have been encountering people of other faiths. The notion that all religions involve an encounter with the same transcendent being is simply not something these pastors or missionaries testify to. What many missionaries do often encounter within the non-Christian communities where they serve, however, is a deep involvement in the occult. It is not rare for this involvement to stretch back over many generations, whilst imprisoning people in great fear in the present. Rather than discovering that contact with the supernatural is simply another expression of the 'cosmic Christ', converts to Christianity from these other religious backgrounds invariably experience something radically different. Confession, repentance and renunciation of past practices become the order of the day.

Prophecy Today, a UK based Christian magazine, incorporates the testimony of a very devout Muslim mystic, Fatima, whose testimony we summarise through the following excerpts:

> Her zeal exceeded that of her parents. As the mark of a true Muslim believer, Fatima swathed herself from head to toe so that no man could look upon her and be tempted. '*I thought I had to be a fanatic,*' she says, '*because I loved God*'.
> She followed the Koran and tried to please Allah by praying more than five times a day. '*I had to do my prayers perfectly*', she states. After her final prayers at night she would supplicate herself thirteen times with her forehead on the floor and recite verses from the Koran.
> While she was still a teenager her family lived in a house with a reputation for being haunted. '*The house itself was demon possessed.*', she says. '*The spirits lived on the second floor. In the night we would hear the furniture moving by itself. So my father locked the rooms and prevented us from going up there. But I was very curious – I*

liked to know about everything. So I went up and was praying and reciting suras against the spirits'.

Fatima entered the forbidden part of the house, sat down and began to draw a picture. It was of Satan. Before long she felt a presence. *'I saw someone beside me wearing a white robe. All my body was trembling'.*

In her alarm, Fatima gathered her things and ran downstairs, but could not bring herself to get rid of the drawing.

'From that time I started to hear voices calling me from the second floor. After that they started to appear in my dreams – increasingly.' And while all the family could hear the furniture moving in the haunted room upstairs it was only Fatima who could hear the voices. The spirits told her they wanted to increase her powers by getting her to recite specific verses from the Koran using them almost as spells ... Fatima tried to resist them but the visions became more alarming. *'They threatened to kill me, to make my husband divorce me. They put words on my tongue. My tongue was moving alone saying, "I want a divorce, I want a divorce" until at last I forced him to divorce me.'*

But even then the spirits would not leave her alone. *'They continued to follow me, saying, "We want you; you have to follow us and you have to work in this way, otherwise we will kill your elder son."'* Fatima's blood ran cold and after this her elder son did become ill. *'In a vision the spirit dug a grave and he brought the child. I was afraid.'*

Continuing with her testimony Fatima relates that in turning to a Christian pastor for help she was led to Christ as her Saviour. Speaking of the burning of the picture of Satan which she had drawn and the deliverance from unclean spirits, she comments upon her belief that there is a spiritual power behind Islam:

'I am sure about that – I don't just believe. I had some Muslim spirits. Those demons used to ... kneel before me and say they are ready to serve me.'

But Fatima can now see the truth: the spirits do not serve us, they make us their slaves.

'If you allow them, they come to you and give you power, and do whatever you ask of them, for healing or hurting people. But what really happens is that the spirits take power and control over those who seek to use them.'[16]

Set against the backdrop of the occult, and the reality of the demonic and destructive bondage of evil spirits, the notion that all religious 'experiences' are manifestations of the same cosmic spirit is surely not tenable. Any theory of comparative religion that suggests unclean spirits are simply an alternative manifestation of God's Holy Spirit cannot expect to be taken seriously.

Turning to so-called experts on world religion as a source of authority here is of little help. The Bible has its own truth-claims to make *vis à vis* comparative religions, and it is these claims which comport with the missionary experience. Central to this perspective on other faiths is the radical need for a powerful work of the Holy Spirit that enables the converts to break free from the dominion of darkness, and transfers them to the kingdom of light.

(f) *Philosophy of Religion for Non-Thinkers*

Connected with all the above is a philosophy of religion which simply flies in the face of reality. Certainly it is possible to establish common denominators of some kind between human beings as spiritual persons. For example, at the most basic level it could be argued that a religious 'experience' is fundamental to followers of all religions. Regardless of the differences between religions they all involve some consciousness or awareness of a spiritual dimension to life. The desire to experience this spiritual dimension is again fundamental to all religious worship. By means of this type of analysis it is possible to establish broad-based denominators common to all religions.

While it is true to say, though, that all adherents of religion have certain things in common, this is no more informative than the observation that all religious people exhibit such common denominators as the desire to live in houses, or to eat food.

The fact that all religious people exhibit a desire to transcend to a spiritual realm does not provide any warrant for the assertion made by pluralists that in reality all religious experiences are basically the same, or simply variations on a theme.

Furthermore, it can easily be established that many people who do profess religious convictions do not in fact share the same philosophy of religion as the religious pluralists. Nor, of course, does the Bible share this. According to the Bible, on becoming a Christian a person is not simply testifying to a religious experience. Christian conversion as such is a distinctive experience which involves certain beliefs, while additionally requiring a certain response to those beliefs. Such beliefs and requirements are exclusive to the Christian faith. For example, someone who claims to have had an experience of God which did not involve what the Bible calls 'repentance' and 'faith' in relation to the person and work of Christ, cannot testify to the same religious experience as the Christian. The religious experience of the Christian has an entire set of characteristics which are an integral part of the encounter with God. Additionally, the Christian understanding of this religious experience is that anything lacking these distinctives cannot be a saving experience.

Thus the Christian experience, whilst being a religious one, is nonetheless a distinctive and exclusive experience. It is not an experience which can be divested of certain claims about the uniqueness of Christ, or the sinfulness of man. It is these claims which have to be understood, believed and responded to in order for the experience to be an authentic and saving one. The philosophy of religion espoused by religious pluralists is one which ignores and dispenses with these realities and claims. It is hardly surprising that anyone who takes the trouble to engage in critical thinking on the subject, will evidence a great deal of disquiet about a philosophy of religion which, while being considered politically correct, is at one and the same time at odds with reality.

Regardless of its illusory epistemological base, however, religious pluralism and the inter-faith movement exist and function as a contemporary threat to the vitality and reality of the Great Commission mandate.

CHAPTER SIX

Ecumenism: *Evangelicals and Catholics together*

Caught up in the great redemptive wave of modern missions are significant areas of the globe traditionally under the influence of Roman Catholicism. Latin America, for example, has witnessed huge numbers of Roman Catholics turning to Christ. Released from dependence upon the sacraments as a means of entry into the kingdom of God such former Catholics are now worshipping God in spirit and truth. Would it not be thrilling indeed to calculate precisely what proportion of today's evangelical church is made up of those who once considered themselves to be trusting in the Roman Catholic faith as a means of salvation. Great numbers, perhaps. This should not come as a surprise to us, since we read in the Scriptures:

> And without faith it is impossible to please Him for he who comes to God must believe that He is and that He is a rewarder of those who seek Him (Heb. 11:6).

God will be found by those whose search is genuine. This is good news for those who, despite all their religious exertions, still feel 'weary and heavy laden' and 'poor in spirit'. Roman Catholics who are genuinely seeking God will surely not be disappointed in their search.

That is not to say that the teachings and influence of Catholicism as such will introduce everyone to a saving faith in Christ. As Alister McGrath has pointed out, a great deal of what passes for Christianity is nothing more than a 'pathetic distortion'. In this context he writes,

> If I could draw upon my own experience as an apologist there seems to be nothing like Roman Catholic boarding schools for turning out committed atheists.[17]

Writing of the growth of the evangelical movement within Latin America, Patrick Johnstone makes the following comment on Chile,

> Possibly one quarter of the population is now affiliated with an evangelical group.[18]

These figures are quite staggering. Johnstone goes on to speak of the significant exodus of Catholics to the evangelical church.

Yet, despite these thrilling testimonies, a movement has gathered pace within evangelical circles which, if heeded, would cause us to weaken or abandon this missionary concern for traditional Roman Catholic people-groups. Charles Colson of Prison Fellowship Ministries is a pivotal evangelical voice in this regard. As most of the evangelical world will now be aware March 1994 saw the production and circulation of a somewhat controversial document commonly referred to as the Colson-Neuhaus Declaration, or the ECT (Evangelicals and Catholics Together) document. It is this document more than any other in recent years that has sparked off a renewed debate concerning the relationship of the Roman Catholic church to the evangelical faith.

When all is said and done, the central question that has to be answered relates to the status of the Roman Catholic church. Given the existing differences between professing evangelicals and Catholics we must surely ask the following question:

Is the Roman Catholic church (i) a 'true' church which preaches the 'true' gospel, but nonetheless has a significant amount of doctrinal error, or (ii) a 'false' church which preaches a 'false' gospel, but nonetheless has a significant degree of doctrinal truth?

Admittedly, one could reject the possibility of answering the question, insisting that the Roman Catholic church is in such a state of flux that no general answer could be given. Perhaps it could be said that there is no single, contemporary voice representing the Roman Catholic church.

However, the need to provide criteria for distinguishing a true from a false church does not seem to have any meaningful place in the ECT scheme of things. Rather, according to the ECT document self-ascription is the key to a church's inclusion within the family of God. In short, if a church claims to enjoy a shared experience of Christ it is to be regarded as genuinely Christian, despite any number of deviant beliefs. The general thrust of the document is towards the forging of a common partnership between those who claim to be evangelicals and those who claim to be Roman Catholic. This common partnership is predicated upon the notion that we all enjoy a shared experience of Christ, regardless of our different doctrinal expressions of it. Indeed, the document goes much wider than this, and speaks of the incorporation of non-evangelical protestant bodies into this broad Christian coalition.

Given the great volume of literature written in opposition to and also in defence of the ECT statement, the comments below touch on concerns about the document's potential impact on Great Commission issues only. Caution is required, though, when addressing the status of the Roman Catholic church at this time in its history. Many of us as protestant evangelicals bring a great deal of baggage with us when we comment on Roman Catholicism. Within such a climate discussing the ECT document becomes very thorny indeed. We would do well to keep at least the following two points in mind as we look at the issues:

i) It would be wrong to deny the fact that evangelical analysis of the Roman Catholic church has at times been marred by extremely imbalanced approaches to the subject matter. Perhaps this is one of the main reasons why the ECT working group has tended to look for a fresh start to the whole debate. This sentiment one can sympathise with. Not all viewpoints expressed on the nature and teachings of the Roman Catholic church have been scholarly, balanced or discerning.

ii) It is perhaps in the Roman Catholic schools rather than non-denominational ones that we are to encounter a basically Christian perspective on moral issues such as abortion, euthanasia and homosexuality.

With that preface, the following considerations may be of value where the ECT document or its implications touch upon the Great Commission.

1. Common Worldview?

As stated at the outset the general thrust of the ECT document is towards a forging of common ground between evangelicals and Catholics. The consolidation of this partnership, it is envisaged, would enlarge the influence of the Church on critical social, political and ethical issues. In so doing a bulwark would be provided against the threat of an increasingly secular political system with its concomitant worldview. In short we recognise that as Roman Catholics and Evangelicals we share the same view on a number of fundamental issues *vis à vis* the nature of and correct ordering of society. In view of this fact, it is held, we can surely cooperate together, thereby presenting a united front on crucial moral issues. The sanctity-of-life principle based upon man being created in the image of God is a fundamental bedrock upon which we are united.

Now it is difficult to imagine a reasonably balanced person objecting to this ecumenical exhortation. All concerned citizens regardless of their religious affiliation surely ought to seek the right ordering of society along the best possible lines. Whatever our denomination, none of us wish to live in a society which is built upon non-Christian or anti-Christian values. Indeed one does not need to be religious at all to perceive that a society based on Christian principles is far more desirable than one erected upon rival social and political philosophies. One of the great strengths of the Reformed faith has been its insistence that the Church has a cultural mandate to reform society in general, as well as a great commission mandate to see the world come to saving faith in Christ.

It is to say the least unfortunate that for many years fundamentalist Christians and other evangelical pietistic groups within western Christianity have simply disengaged from any social interface with society at the level of Christian ethics. Emphasis has been placed almost entirely on our being pilgrims on our way to Heaven, who need not engage in earthly affairs. The result of this disengagement has been a marginalisation of the evangelical church within society as a whole. Believing the world to be a sinking ship, we have all but abandoned society to the influence of any one of several non- or anti-Christian worldviews. Given this socio-political backdrop to the ECT document the emphasis upon a concerted voice in favour of commonly shared Christian values is a most welcome exhortation. On ethical questions such as human sexuality and the sanctity of life we can indeed speak with one voice.

A cultural mandate to restructure society in line with our commonly shared values is surely a powerful aspiration which few of us can afford to dismiss.

2. *Common Faith?*

If this were all that the ECT paper was recommending, then one would have no reason to be anything other than encouraged. The grave danger, however, with this particular document is that a recognition of having 'commonly shared values' is somehow equated with the idea that both Evangelicals and Roman Catholics are actually 'confessors of the same faith' and 'preachers of the same gospel'.

How does one respond to such a claim? It is extremely difficult to do so adequately in such a general chapter as this. Perhaps one could simply cite the testimonies of those converts to Christ who formerly were Roman Catholics themselves.

Sitting in front of me is a thrilling book entitled, *The Truth Set Us Free* by Richard Bennet. The book is a wonderful compilation of the testimonies of twenty former nuns who have come to Christ though the truth of the gospel. Certainly these testimonies would appear to be at loggerheads with the 'discovery' testified to in the ECT document. Indeed the witness of these ladies heads in quite the opposite direction from the ECT document. In the one we are being told that the great 'discovery' which the contributors made was that we are all one in Christ. Now here is a book of testimonies where Roman Catholic sisters have made the exact opposite discovery.

Peggy O'Neil served as a sister in a religious order for about fifty years and writes of this time:

> I served as a sister in a religious order for about fifty years and during that time I never heard the true Gospel.[19]

This testimony is repeated again and again where the truth of Scripture is absent within a religious system of man-made regulations. Richard Bennett, who edits the book, and who was a Roman Catholic priest for twenty one years, suggests that the book will be of avid interest to:

> evangelicals who are being drawn more closely into 'dialogue' with Roman Catholics, unaware of the inner workings of that huge, seemingly mysterious system.[20]

It seems difficult in the light of this sort of testimony to lay a great deal of store by the notion that we are all in reality preaching the same gospel.

Leaving aside the notion of testimonies, one could surely list the teachings of Roman Catholicism as contained within the official and authoritative sources of the church, and compare these teachings with the claims of Holy Scripture. Time-consuming yes – but fairly straightforward. Given a reasonable grasp of the issues, it should be possible to distinguish a false from a true church if the criteria for doing so were put in place.

Now once again it is essential not to weaken the evangelical position by overstating things. It will do little good to the cause of evangelicalism if our response to this document is to suggest that there are no common theological convictions or notions which stretch across the divide. However, that is not at all the same as insisting that both church traditions are preaching identical gospel messages.

It should also be mentioned that not everyone would lay great store by the procedure of piling up theological common denominators as indicators of possible unity. Given that Christianity is a 'system' of truth, one should compare overall systems rather than isolated doctrines.

Whatever approach we take to the ECT claims, it surely remains far-fetched to maintain that on pivotal issues such as salvation by faith alone, and Scripture alone as our authority, we are all really saying the same thing, just using different words.

3. *Common Vision?*

Clearly, an acceptance of the idea that both faiths are preaching the same message leads inexorably to the conclusion reached or implied within the document itself, namely: that all missionary efforts aimed at Roman Catholic people groups are not really necessary (Section 5, We Witness Together). This for the simple reason that evangelical missionaries are simply telling Roman Catholic people about a gospel which they have already embraced. In short, we are preaching to the converted; and evangelism is thus by implication no more than sheep-stealing.

However for many missionaries serving within the world of Roman Catholicism and indeed, as previously noted, for great numbers of converted Roman Catholics, the Colson-Neuhaus 'discovery' that we are all in fact Christians anyway has an air or unreality about it. Let us, though, for the sake of argument momentarily accept and embrace the general idea contained within the ECT paper: namely; that we are indeed all of the one faith. Given this astonishing discovery, perhaps someone could well ask the question as to why evangelical missionary work within the Roman Catholic world would thereafter constitute a problem for the Roman Catholic church? What could all the fuss be about if there is no distinction to be made between the gospel messages of the two communities?

If, as the ECT document asserts, we are all aiming to spread the same faith by the preaching of the same biblical gospel, then surely the presence of protestant missionaries, preachers and evangelists in traditional Catholic communities would be welcomed by the Roman Catholic church? Catholics recognising their need to turn to Christ in repentance and faith; minds being renewed; the Bible being prayerfully studied; families being transformed and God being worshipped in spirit and truth – is not this something which according to the ECT signatories we would jointly rejoice over?

If on the other hand this is not the response one receives from the Roman Catholic church over a sinner who repents and finds newness of life, then perhaps the ECT agenda should focus more on the cultural mandate which allows for common ground on shared values, and abandon the semantic gymnastics surrounding their attempt to evangelise the world by definitional conversions rather than real ones!

(4) *Common Missiology?*

A further problem arises, though, in connection with the Great Commission. It is not at all clear that the Great Commission is on the agenda of the Roman Catholic church! According to Vatican II (1962-65) the church's view of non-Christian religions is such that Buddhists, Muslims, Hindus and others can all be saved anyway, regardless of whether or not they hear the gospel. In other words non- Christian religions provide ways of salvation. A common vision in respect of the Great Commission does not seem to be on the agenda!

In conclusion, it seems that two grave errors are to be avoided:

First, we must dismiss the notion that there are no common bonds with Catholicism and hence no broad Christian coalition possible on a single-issue basis, such as pro-life. Secondly, one would simply be engaging in denial to insist that at this point in history the way of salvation found within each of our traditions is the same.

CHAPTER SEVEN

Wideness in God's Mercy

Many Christians are familiar with the heroic and indomitable spirit which has characterised the modern missionary movement. Some have been martyred, leaving behind heartbroken loved ones; others have willingly placed their children in missionary schools, being united as a family only once or twice a year; countless numbers have been struck down by disease or in some other way been called upon to endure hardship and deprivation. Indigenous evangelists have died of starvation in labour camps simply because they insisted on evangelising those who had not heard the gospel. National Christians prayerfully and reflectively look back and thank God for the day that the Holy Spirit compelled another to bring them a message, the result of which was deliverance from the kingdom of darkness.

The situation has not changed today. All over the world 'commissioning' services are taking place as men, women and children dedicate themselves to a future of deprivation and danger in order to attempt to reach the remaining unevangelised peoples of the planet.

For those who gave, and continue to give, so much for the cause of Christ amidst the nations, and for those who rejoiced at deliverance by the gospel, the adherents of the Wider Hope theory have but one question: What was all the fuss about?

This rather fashionable school of thought which is now being popularised as an evangelical option functions as a kind of Copernican Revolution in missionary thinking. Unfortunately the stakes are much higher and the cogency of the reasoning behind the argument far less convincing. It is, though, a politically correct message, and should it be embraced by evangelicals widely it may well provide Christianity with instant acceptance by the world. No evangelical armed with this viewpoint need feel socially awkward ever again.

General Idea of the Wider Hope Theory

Whilst there are variations within this school of thought, the general idea is that from a judicial point of view only Christ's righteousness through his death and resurrection can secure an individual's salvation. We know this because the Bible teaches it. So far so good. However as far as the unevangelised are concerned, there need be no worry, since it is in fact not at all necessary for a person to respond to this message, or indeed even hear about it. God will simply accept the plea of an individual for mercy, it is held, and require nothing beyond that. Unlike religious pluralism, Wider Hope belief does not hold that an individual can be saved by their religion, but rather a person may be saved within and perhaps despite their own religious worldview. The originality of this theory rests in the assertion that one does not need to *respond* to anything of the person and work of Christ to be saved. Thus we have a world full of 'anonymous Christians'.

No one should doubt the growing strength of this viewpoint. Rev. John Brand who is currently the UK Director for the Africa Inland Mission reports with alarm in the October 1999 editorial of the A.I.M. magazine:

> An evangelical journal of theology article entitled 'Those Who Have Never Heard' concluded with these sentiments:
> 'I feel that a sincere believer in the one true Creator God may possibly be saved apart from explicit knowledge of the gospel of Christ ... Possibly even some of the unevangelised "heathen" of centuries past are among the elect who will be found in heaven.'

John Brand responds in the A.I.M. magazine with the following:

> That such statements should come from a reputedly evangelical stable illustrate just how much ambivalence there is about the biblical teaching on the plight of the unreached. Wishful thinking and sentiment have replaced God's Word as the objective authority and touchstone of belief.

This argument, though, of anonymous Christians appears to have a type of Solomon-like wisdom, since it upholds the claim for the uniqueness of Christ's propitiatory sacrifice as the only grounds of salvation, yet avoids the unpleasant conclusion that without actually responding to this claim a person cannot be saved. In this way we appear to have the best of both worlds. Certainly there would have been many occasions in New Testament times when such information would have brought great comfort to the infant Church charged with the responsibility of fulfilling the Great Commission. Indeed, as the Christian community came into contact with the multi-faith society of the Roman Empire one would have expected to find wider hope assertions scattered throughout the New Testament.

The questions we need to address, though, are: can these incredible assertions actually be true? and, if yes, how are such conclusions reached? Difficulties with the Wider Hope theory abound, and one need not reflect a great deal before stumbling upon some of the more obvious. The key complaint which has given rise to this belief is important here, namely that someone, somewhere will be denied the justice due to them on the day of judgement. Wider Hope belief seeks to solve that apparent problem. We shall deal with the biblical position on the matter of justice shortly, but first we must consider some reasons for disquiet concerning the reasonableness of the Wider Hope theory.

1. *A Doctrine of Silence*
Given the wide range of theological issues which this complex set of beliefs impacts, the precise definitions called for and indeed the possible eternal implications for mankind, we would rightfully expect to find in defence of this position a degree of justification from the Bible second to none. After all, we are speaking of a revolution in Christian theology. The burden of proof, therefore, would appear to rest very firmly upon the shoulders of those making such assertions to provide a highly persuasive warrant for the astonishing claims being made.

Oddly enough a problem is encountered right at this point, and it is one which many of us would not expect to find. The Bible, we are told, is 'silent' on the subject. Or if you like, the fate of the unevangelised is never directly addressed in Scripture. Now even a person of modest intellect could be forgiven for feeling slightly ill at ease at this point. A complex range of theological assertions constructed upon a doctrine of silence? These are not impressive credentials. There is surely something rather counter-intuitive about a range of theological assertions for which an absence of biblical evidence is the *sine qua non* of the argument. Ought we not to be forgiven for expecting something more than this?

These things notwithstanding, what we do know is that for those who are passionately consumed with taking the gospel to the unreached we have here a message which promises the calming effect of an expensive cigar. In a word, things are not quite as desperate as we thought they were. In the last analysis there is no real urgency about taking the gospel message to the unreached, since the unreached may be saved without responding to or being confronted with the message of the gospel. This is apparently the good news.

Now to be fair to those who hold to this position, most would not wish to suggest that we cease taking the gospel to the unreached. It is simply that we can no longer think of any ultimate reason for doing so. Perhaps it is also only fair to point out that the idea of the Bible being silent on the fate of those who are unevangelised does not ring true with everyone else. In fact many ordinary people are convinced that the Scriptures have a very great deal to say on the issue, and for that reason dedicate themselves to some form of evangelistic outreach.

For the present we simply note the claim that for the unevangelised to be saved they do not need to hear, respond to or obey the requirements of the gospel message. Now once again it must be said that if this were true it would be an extremely reassuring message.

2. *Ambiguous Definitions*

Despite these words of comfort, any speculation as to who in particular may draw strength from this viewpoint immediately encounters difficulties. A number of terms are actually employed by adherents of this position, each one of which is alas susceptible to a whole host of different meanings, interpretations and definitions. Thus a wide-ranging of classifications and explanations (e.g. 'unevangelised'; 'those who won't hear'; 'the untold'; 'those who cannot hear') is to be found scattered like dice throughout this school of thought. Unfortunately such user-friendly vagueness is not a propitious attribute for any theory of moral philosophy, since it leaves us guessing at who precisely is included in this scheme of things, and what the criteria happen to be for one's inclusion.

Perhaps the safest definition would involve the idea of someone who 'through no fault of their own' has never been confronted with the claims of the gospel. This is the type of general wording normally associated with Wider Hope theories.

3. *Confusing Application*

The problem with this type of wording i.e. 'through no fault of their own' is that it does not admit of any clear and unambiguous application. For example, it would be very difficult to make a moral distinction between those who 'through no fault of their own' are denied a hearing of the gospel for reasons of geography, from those such as, for example, Muslims who 'through no fault of their own' are misled about the gospel. The former have no one to tell them the gospel, while the latter draw back from taking the opportunity to investigate it, because they have previously been deceived into thinking it is harmful.

Would Wider Hope advocates really have us believe that millions of Muslims who, misled by the teachings of the Koran, openly reject the historical death, resurrection, saving work and deity of Christ, but cast themselves upon God for mercy, may still be saved by that which they deny? Truth expressed in error? Unbelief experienced as saving faith? Denial transformed into profession? Mosques full of born again Muslims? Can this really be true!

Not that the ambiguity stops with those who 'through no fault of their own' are misled, or denied the gospel. Consider, for example, those who do hear the gospel, yet through no fault of their own forget the message, or are confused about the message. Or what of those who do not sense any need for the gospel, and so simply do not bother asking any questions?

In the light of the above scenarios, and doubtless the many more which could be constructed, it should be clear that Wider Hope theories cannot remain restricted to the odd community stranded on a desert island without e-mail or radio contact. Once examined the theories admit of unwieldy, terribly general and rather confusing application.

If the doctrine of evangelism is so fraught with complexity and confusion one is left to wonder why the New Testament writers did not even allude to such.

4. *Lightweight Apologetics*

If we are so easily confused about the application of the Wider Hope theory, then there is even less satisfaction when presented with attempted justifications for Wider Hope claims. Daniel B. Clendenin in his book, *Many Gods Many Lords* (Baker Books, 1995), lists what he considers a five point presentation of the most important points for inclusivism i.e. the belief that one can be saved by Christ without hearing of Christ. It may be helpful to provide a brief critique of each point. (It should be noted that Clendenin is not necessarily advocating the points but simply explaining and highlighting them.)

The *first* controlling belief in the inclusivist scheme of things is the apparent discovery of a *paradox* between God's universality (He loves all people) and particularity (He reconciles sinners through Jesus' mediation alone).

The combination of these two facts, according to Wider Hope advocates, forms a dialectical truth. That is to say, the truths of universality and particularity stand in opposition to each other. But from these two opposites a synthesis will ultimately emerge. Thus the defence of the inclusivist position begins with the discovery of a problem i.e. God claims to love all people, but will save people only through Christ. And these two truths, we are told, stand in opposition to each other.

For many people, though, this apparent problem is quite simply an imaginary one. There is no *paradox* or *dialectic* at work here. Yes it true that God loves and will save people from every tribe, nation and tongue; and it is equally true that the person and work of Christ is the means whereby this will be accomplished. Indeed as has been pointed out, this is precisely what is happening in today's world as people respond to the claims of the gospel. These two truths, then, rather than constituting a problem, present us with a solution.

The notion that the relationship between God's love on the one hand, and the nature and scope of Christ's redemptive work on the other, is somehow paradoxical or dialectic, is certainly not taken from the top drawer of apologetics. A paradox happens when apparent *contradictions* coincide in the same truth-claim. The problem with this paradox is that it does not really exist.

The *second* argument in favour of inclusivism involves a philosophical dissecting of Christ's saving work. According to this argument we must distinguish between the *ontological* and the *epistemological* aspects of Christ's redemptive work. The ontological aspect of Christ's work functions as the grounds of redemption and is quite crucial. However the epistemological aspect deals with information about the saving work of Christ. This, we are told, does not have the same importance attached to it. As long as we hold on to the ontological grounds of salvation we can relax our insistence about the epistemological side of things. Clendenin writes:

> ... inclusivists also distinguish between the ontological necessity of the work of Christ and the epistemological necessity of hearing about and responding to it in an explicitly cognitive manner...[21]

There is little need for anyone to be concerned that something profound is being held up for consideration at this point. The introduction of *ontological* and *epistemological* necessities does not add anything to the discussion since this is simply a fancy way of repeating the same old claim i.e. that Christ's death provides the grounds of salvation, but actually hearing about this is not necessary.

It may be worthwhile noting, though, in response to this

ontology/epistemology division that in actual fact the gospel involves much more than this. What seems to have been overlooked in this compartmentalising of the gospel is that the Christian message is ethical in character and as such has a moral claim upon mankind. The gospel is not just a passing on of information, but rather involves a moral confrontation requiring an obedient response. It is for this reason that the word *obedience* is often included in the expected and appropriate response to the proclamation of the gospel.

By reducing the idea of conversion to a simple cognitive awareness of Christ the impression given is that the only thing standing before an otherwise perfectly good religious person and salvation is a slight shortfall in theological awareness. That is to say that apart from this information it would be possible for someone to meet all other conditions necessary for acceptance before God.

However, as anyone even remotely familiar with the New Testament will be aware, any response to the gospel involves something more than simple cognisance of its claims. Throughout the world great numbers of people identify cognitively with Christ. Nominal church-goers do so every week. This, though, is not the same as conversion. Conversion involves a moral confrontation with and ethical response to the claims of Christ, the result of which is a Holy Spirit-empowered repentance. It is this moral response – experienced as conviction and expressed in repentance and conversion – which is a prerequisite to a person's acceptance before God.

Alongside the above line of argument Clendenin also mentions an analogy drawn by inclusivists which seems to indicate that similar ground has already been conceded concerning those who have not been made aware of the gospel message. Speaking of situations analogous to those raised by the Wider Hope theory he writes:

> We observed in chapter 1 that many Christians would readily affirm such a statement in regard to people who lived before Christ, infants who die, retarded people who do not have the mental capability to understand the gospel, and people who have no opportunity to hear

the gospel. Inclusivists simply extend by analogy to these four examples salvation of people of other religions.[22]

Extending the analogy of *infants who die* to *those of other religions* is doubtless very tempting, but precisely what justification exists for doing so is not at all clear. One cannot legitimately extend an analogy by simply desiring to do so. In order for an analogy to exist we must have two things which are in the same logical category.

The Christian Church has historically considered infants and those with brain disorders as being in a category which renders them incapable of making a rational response to the gospel. In order for any analogy to be drawn to any other category of person it would require that the person be like those just mentioned i.e. lacking in rational capacity or ability to respond to the gospel. Given that adults within other religions are perfectly capable of rational comprehension, it is simply nonsense to insist that they are in the same logical category as those such as infants who lack the capacity to make an intelligent response to the gospel.

One could be forgiven for thinking that we are once again being presented with a theory which has 'Alice in Wonderland' qualities. In other words the analogy, like the earlier paradox, would appear to be at best illusory.

In response to this objection Wider Hope advocates suggest that the analogy actually relates to a lack of *opportunity* rather than a lack of rational ability. However, in this case one can only repeat that (a) capacity and opportunity are not the same, and (b) people do not incur judgement for not having the opportunity to hear the gospel; they are justly judged in connection with their present response to the general revelation already before them.

Injecting into this analogy the observation that some Christians believe that those who have no opportunity to hear the gospel and those who lived before Christ will be saved, is really begging the question. The warrant for any theological truth-claim is not provided by a contemporary description of who happens to believe what. The real question is whether or not this argument comports with the teaching of God's Word. That is not to say that theological consensus from the perspective of church history is not significant. However, such a perspective would provide small comfort for 'inclusivists', since the history of the Church provides little support for this view.

The *third* point highlighted by Clendenin comes to us in the form of the following question:

> Does it stand to reason that God would so clearly express his universal salvic intentions, procure that salvation through the particular costly death of his only Son and then make salvation accessible only to a tiny minority?

In contrast with this sentiment God in His Word would appear to place emphasis on the expressing of gratitude for that which he has accomplished. The reason for this unceasing gratitude is, of course, that there is not one single person among us who deserves to be saved. The Bible simply does not envisage that mankind will have a complaint in this regard.

It may be worth making at this point an interesting observation from church history. Within the course of western Christianity it has been possible to keep fairly accurate written accounts of seasons of revival. That is to say, it is possible to discover the circumstances surrounding particular occasions when God in great power manifested his glory. He did so, for example, to segments of the populations of the United Kingdom and North America in an unusual way. We are thinking here of the Great Awakening in the time of Whitefield and Edwards in the 1740s and the second, though lesser known, American awakening which lasted twenty five years, from 1800–1825 (see *Revival and Revivalism,* Iain H. Murray, Banner of Truth, 1994). Awakenings are important for this particular discussion in that it is on such occasions that God seems to draw near to man in unusually powerful ways. The impression God as creator makes upon man as the created will be instructive for us.

Two points concerning revival are significant in relation to Clendenin's question:

(a) All great religious awakenings have certain common

denominators. The experience of a deep sense of sin before a holy God is an accompanying and distinguishing mark of revival.

As far as can be ascertained, there is no record of any revival, the result of which leads to people expressing a grievance concerning the injustice of God's plan of salvation. Indeed, precisely the opposite is the case. Individuals who lie prostrate before the awesomeness of God tend to experience a deep sense of unworthiness in respect of salvation. When people are confronted with the awesomeness and holiness of God it produces the conviction that no one deserves to be saved at all. A profound gratitude for God's grace in respect of salvation is present.

(b) Another consequence of earlier religious awakenings is the manifestation of a deep concern to bring the gospel to those who are lost.

The spontaneous creation of missionary societies to reach the lost is a recorded fruit of revival. Once again this powerful encounter with God tends to set people's hearts in a different direction to that of today's *avant-garde* missiologists, such as John Hick. It would be very difficult indeed to produce any record of revival which was accompanied by a conviction that man generally did not need to hear the gospel to be saved. On the contrary, such aberrant views tend to evaporate following powerful encounters with God.

Within the context of the complaint Clendenin also records dissatisfaction on the part of inclusivists concerning the scope and representative nature of the work of redemption. Salvation is restricted to a 'tiny minority'. Once again it is noteworthy that within the context of revival this type of thinking evaporates.

Speaking of the Great Revival of the eighteenth century, and its impact on world-wide evangelisation, Iain Murray records in his internationally acclaimed book, *The Puritan Hope:*

> The evangelical revival in the English-speaking world two hundred years ago had a vast influence in increasing confidence that all the nations of the earth would yet be turned to the gospel of Christ.[23]

Lest we should consider that this was only optimistic thinking, Murray further comments:

In and after the 1790s there arose in Britain a series of new missionary societies which were to be so strongly supported that for more than a century Britain was to remain in the foremost place in the world-wide spread of true Christianity.[24]

Once again the significance here is that these developments all took place within the context of revival. God had drawn near to man in powerful operations of his Spirit. As a result thousands of converts were deeply moved by the impression that not only did the nations need to hear the gospel, but the task could actually be accomplished. In all of this they were at one with the great expectations contained within the Scriptures themselves:

> After this I looked and there before me was a great multitude which no man could count, from every nation, tribe, people and language, standing before the throne and in front of the Lamb. They were wearing white robes and were holding palm branches in their hands. And they cried out in a loud voice:
>
> > 'Salvation belongs to our God who sits on the throne, and to the Lamb' (Rev. 7:9, 10).

Apparently puzzled at this worship of God by the above throng, inclusivists, we are told, understand this eventual proportion of saved to unsaved mankind as being at variance with something called 'moral logic'. The general idea is that somehow a greater return should be expected from Christ's sacrificial death on the cross. One is not sure at this point whether the complaint is that Christ has been short-changed by the low return, or that mankind has in fact been sold short by the limited nature of Christ's death. Whatever the conclusion it is quite at variance with the messianic passages of Isaiah the prophet. Of the sufferings of Christ we read:

> He shall see the labour of His soul and be satisfied.
> By His knowledge My righteous Servant shall justify many,
> For He shall bear their iniquities (Is. 53:11).

In response to the above complaints concerning the limited scope of saving grace it would not be disingenuous to suggest that rather than feel the force of the Wider Hope argument, many may be more inclined to recall the words of Job. Speaking of the sinful and perverted tendency within man to call upon God to give an account for his actions, Job says:

> Will the faultfinder contend with the Almighty? Let him who reproves God answer it (Job 40:1, 2).

Only God as sovereign judge of the universe has the authority to make moral judgements on such issues. Only God can specify the value placed on the redemption of the Church. It would, therefore, seem ill-advised to suggest – as Wider Hope theorists do – that there is room here for not just a complaint, but a complaint grounded in an appeal to justice. Clendenin comments:

> This is an appeal based not upon mere sentiment or emotion as is sometimes charged but an appeal based upon the revealed character of God and the standards of justice and right that he has implanted in our minds and hearts.[25]

Perhaps, though, Shakespeare had a better grasp of the issues:

> Though justice be thy plea consider this; that in the course of justice none of us should see salvation (Merchant of Venice).

As Shakespeare rightly observes, making a plea for *justice* is not the wisest course of action to take when approaching God. Presenting the plea by way of a complaint about who is getting what may be even more ill-advised. However, to engage God on the subject of *rights* at all in respect of salvation is entirely out of the question. No one of us has a right to grace, or to mercy. No one has a right to be saved. Such perverted notions, rather than reflect standards which God has placed within our hearts, may be better diagnosed as symptoms of a mind-set that should never be there in the first place. Indeed, as Jeremiah reveals, the thoughts of our heart do not provide a reliable plumb-line by which to gauge anyone's actions, far less God's.

> The heart is deceitful above all things,
> and desperately corrupt; who can understand it? (Jer. 17:9).

The *fourth* point highlighted by Clendenin is that the phenomenon of world religious practices is not entirely negative, may well be ambiguous, and can in fact be full of truth, beauty, grace and goodness.

The only possible response to this claim is to ask the question – according to what standard are we determining this truth and goodness? By what plumb-line is the big claim being measured? Certainly no one will dispute any claim within world religion that comports with reality as found within the Word of God.

Should someone believe in monotheism, or assert that God created the universe, the Christian should not have a problem accepting their truth-claims, since all truth is of God. Such general truth, though, is not the same as a saving truth-claim, and it is saving truth in particular that we are expected to believe may be found in other religions.

It must be tempting for Wider Hope advocates to produce their secret weapon at this point, and parade before the world hundreds of converted Muslims, Buddhists, Animists and Hindus testifying to the truth and goodness of their religious experience before and after conversion to Christ. For such testimonies to provide support for the Wider Hope view they would need to sound something like this:

> On turning to Christ for forgiveness of sins I was surprised to find that I had actually been accepted by God all along, and that my previous religious works and aspirations were the ethical fruits of pure and undefiled religion in my life.

However the problem is that contrary to all expectations this is precisely what one does nor hear! Indeed, as the gospel spreads throughout the continents of Asia and Africa it is the opposite testimony which we are hearing. We are hearing that Christ has set people free from forms of religious and spiritual darkness, and has transferred them into a kingdom of light.

The question remains, though, as to the standard according to which all of this has to be judged? Recognising that at some point one has to do a little better than build an argument from silence Wider Hope advocates do make eventual reference to the

Scriptures. However for the most part this recourse to the Bible seems to require a setting aside of the mind, rather than an application of it. Consider the following example. Once again we are indebted to Daniel Clendenin for his reporting. Speaking of other world religions he reminds us that:

> As we observed in chapter two it is not too difficult to find people of non-Christian religions who exhibit what would appear to be the ethical evidences of salvation – righteousness, joy, peace and the like.[26]

Someone may wish to question at this point why we are limiting our observations of such moral qualities to only religious people. Cannot atheists and agnostics also manifest such qualities as patience, concern for others and gentleness? And are we therefore suggesting that these qualities are the fruits of salvation in such lives? Judas Iscariot, it seems, showed remarkable patience and self control as he watched for the best opportunity to betray Christ. Were these the fruits of salvation? The fact is that Christians have never claimed that qualities such as self-control and patience are unique to the Christian. (It should be said here that a professing Christian who evidences none of these qualities has a dubious testimony.)

The significance of these virtues in the life of the Christian goes well beyond the qualities themselves. Their significance and distinctiveness relate to the internal workings of the Holy Spirit, under whose influence and ministry these virtues are produced. This is clearly distinct from other natural causes, like temperament or circumstances. Thus the key issue in respect of apparently mutual virtues present in the life of the Christian and non-Christian concerns not similarity or appearances, but rather authenticity. The key question we must ask is not, 'Is this a patient person?', but rather, 'Is this person's patience being produced due to the saving and sanctifying work of the Holy Spirit?'

Consider the following illustration.

Upon purchasing a painting by Monet we discover that it is actually not an original by Monet but an identical copy produced by another artist. The issue here is not one of *similarity,* in that no matter how close to the original the painting is it is still not a Monet. The painting does not become a Monet even should it be perfected to the degree that only Monet himself could tell the difference. In order for it to be an authentic Monet painting Monet has to be the original artist. Now it is precisely the same when we ask about the nature and source of these ethical qualities. The key question relates to the authenticity of the virtues. Are they being produced as a result of the saving work of the Holy Spirit, or of some other 'artist'?

Clendenin returns again to this issue after citing the convictions of Sir Norman Anderson concerning certain Muslim mystics in their search for God. In some cases, Anderson tells us, this seeking is genuine. This should not strike us as unreasonable, since many converted Muslims tell us that they were searching for God. (The reader may recall the earlier searching of the Muslim mystic Fatima who recalled, 'I thought I had to be a fanatic because I loved God'.)

Clendenin now suggests that, 'Scripture might give some warrant for this point'. What he means, though, is not a warrant for the assertion that people are at times searching for God. Rather, he speaks of a scriptural warrant for the notion that this seeking and its accompanying ethical fruits may well be evidences of salvation.

Now given the startling nature of Clendenin's question, it may be helpful for the reader to return to Fatima's testimony at this point, and re-read the story of this devout Muslim mystic who manifested exactly those qualities described by Clendenin as possible fruits of salvation. Additionally, it might be helpful to recall another section of her testimony. Following a request by her for prayer from the pastor, she recalls:

> They were sitting in a circle and I could see the demon. He was very black, huge and had no eyes. His face was just blank. He was sitting resisting during the prayers until at last the pastor said, 'In the name of Jesus I command you, leave her!' The demon ran out. And then I started to feel a very big stone in my stomach. When they said, 'In the name of Jesus!' it came up and I was about to faint. After that I felt like a mountain was above me and it vanished.[27]

Other demons followed.

These things notwithstanding, Clendenin claims that there may be scriptural warrant for the claim that mystical Muslims (like Fatima) may well be evidencing the fruits of salvation! The scriptural warrant cited is from the book of James. The text is James 1:26, 27 where, speaking of 'pure and undefiled religion', the context reads as follows:

> My dear brothers (v.19) ... Do not merely listen to the word and so deceive yourselves. Do what it says. Anyone who listens to the word but does not do what it says is like a man who looks at his face in a mirror and after looking at it himself goes away and immediately forgets what he looks like. But the man who looks intently into the perfect law that gives freedom and continues to do this, not forgetting what he has heard but doing it – he will be blessed in what he does.
>
> If anyone considers himself religious and yet does not keep a tight rein on his tongue, he deceives himself and his religion is worthless. Religion that God our Father accepts as pure and faultless is this: to look after orphans and widows in their distress and to keep oneself from being polluted by the world (vv.22-27).

Clearly this passage: (a) is addressed to professing Christians, (b) is raising the issue of the need for professing Christians to respond in deed to the teachings of God's Word.

Now the question may be asked: by what possible means can this passage be construed as referring to mystic Muslims? I, for one, have no answer to that. To suggest – as Clendenin seems to – that the book of James, or indeed passages within it, are speaking of religion in general, rather than Christianity in particular, would appear to involve the employment of what Professor Douglas Kelly has entitled in another context *an exegesis of desperation.*[28]

If this is the best biblical reference on offer, Wider Hope advocates or their apologists may be better advised to seek refuge in the insistence that the Bible has nothing to say on the issue at all! Better an argument based on silence than one based on the type of claim that has just been made!

It is worth at this point returning briefly to the vexed question concerning ethical qualities which are to be admired within the person who happens to be very religious, yet does not follow the teachings of Christ. Perhaps it will be helpful to divide such religious persons into two categories:

i) those who manifest ethical uprightness, yet who after careful thought and perhaps for a variety of reasons reject the claims and teachings of Christ.

We are thinking here of the religious individual who is a very devout person seeking to worship God in and through his or her own faith. Such a person may give alms, fast, pray etc just like a Christian, yet reject the total teaching of the Bible on the person, claims and work of Christ. What comment can we make on these otherwise apparently excellent people?

The Scriptures have a whole range of possible answers to this question. Generally speaking, the Bible does not suggest any automatic link between a religious profession and a pure heart. Sometimes devoutly religious individuals can be very insincere people, particularly in a society where religion is highly regarded. However the question here relates to individuals who will perhaps make a statement or claim something like this:

> I have looked into the claims of Christ and genuinely cannot accept these exclusive claims as representing God's perspective on things. Thus the only thing I can do is continue to worship God in my own, or in some other way.

This, of course, is no different a response to the exclusive claims of Christ that of lots of people in New Testament times. Given this fact one can only reply with the same answers formulated at that time by Jesus. Consider the following response to those who were questioning the truth-value of the claims being made by Jesus concerning his representation of truth:

> My teaching is not my own, it comes from him who sent me. If anyone chooses to do God's will he will find out whether my teaching comes from God or whether I speak on my own (John 7:17).

Now these words create a real dilemma. What Christ appears to be implying is that a rejection of his teaching indicates an insincerity in certain religious people's apparent search for God.

Or put another way, Jesus is suggesting that if a person's search for God is genuine, then it must of necessity involve a positive acceptance of Christ's teachings and revelation, since his teachings are true, and actually come from the God people claim they are searching for. Accordingly, there is no such experience as a genuine search for God which involves a rejection of Christ's teachings once understood. The insincerity of the search is thus the answer to the above question.

ii) regardless of a person's relationship to the gospel message, however, what of the ethical qualities which we all recognise as present at times in the Hindu, Buddhist and Muslim? If these are not the fruits of salvation, then what are they?

It is puzzling that this question should be approached as if it were new to the Christian mind. Once again it is good to remind ourselves that ours is not the first generation to address such a question. What is even more encouraging perhaps is that some of the most engaging thinkers in the history of the Church have taken note of this as an issue, and actually formulated widely accepted responses to the subject.

Jonathan Edwards (1703–1758) is regarded by many as America's greatest evangelical philosopher and theologian. John Calvin (1509–1564) is regarded by many as Europe's most brilliant theologian. Neither of these men was unaware of the apparent goodness in those around them who were not converted to Christ. Consequently, in addressing this question the Christian doctrine of 'common grace' was formulated and expounded.

Edwards' *Treatise on Grace* is a stunning commentary on the issue.[29] Calvin tackles the issue in his *Institutes*.[30]

According to the doctrine of *common grace* God by his Holy Spirit can be at work in the lives of individuals, families, and nations in a way which does not result in salvation. These operations of the Holy Spirit can have a multitude of beneficial and desirable results, including the cultivation of virtue and what we all consider natural affection within society. Consequently, it is quite possible to encounter a person who – while claiming to be an atheist, is in every respect more than civil to those around him.

Interestingly, great mileage is sought these days from the notion that many contemporary peoples and cultures still find themselves living in 'Old Testament times'. What are we to say of peoples who live in such times, yet manifest virtues and qualities which we can only admire? The answer would appear to be the Old Testament teaching on common grace!

Fifthly, we are reminded that the *'eschatological judgement belongs to God alone and God has promised to deal justly and mercifully with mankind*'.[31] This exhortation is coupled with the warning that we dare not usurp the divine prerogative.

Certainly with this exhortation and warning one can only be in hearty agreement. Seeking to set aside or add to God's teaching on such ultimate issues as the Great Commission mandate, or the eternal welfare of man, is not a light matter. Moreover the Church has not been left bereft of eschatological information concerning how we are to prepare for this application of justice by God alone.

The Church is very familiar with the warning contained within the book of Revelation:

> I warn everyone who hears the words of the prophecy of this book: If anyone adds anything to these words, God will add to that person the disasters written about in this book. And if anyone takes away from the words of prophecy, God will take away that one's share of the tree of life and of the holy city which are written about in this book (Rev. 22:18).

Adding to, subtracting from or changing God's message, according to the above warnings, is not a good idea.

Into the same category comes the warning not to render unclear or confuse the purposes of God by making claims contrary to truth.

> Who is this that makes my purpose unclear,
> by saying things that are not true? (Job 38:2).

Reviewing the arguments put forward by Wider Hope adherents it is difficult to escape the conclusion that this is exactly what is happening. By disseminating ideas which collide head on with the biblical mandate of the Great Commission, a spiritual confusion is enveloping the Christian Church at this crucial time. Indeed it is the eschatological passages of the Scriptures which more than any other imply a great separation of peoples on the day of judgement. Little comfort can be drawn for the Wider Hope cause by introducing the notion of 'eschatological judgement'. It is this very judgement which renders their arguments nil and void.

5. *Simplistic View of The Gospel*
A further difficulty with Wider Hope speculation is the notion that unevangelised people cannot be guilty of disobeying the gospel, and therefore ought not to be held accountable before God for anything arising from that state of affairs.

Firstly, it should be noted once again that the proclamation of the gospel in the New Testament involves something much more than biographical information about Jesus of Nazareth. The gospel message incorporates moral truth concerning God the Creator's rightful expectations of mankind, while at the same time proclaiming His righteous judgement upon all sin. Contrary to Wider Hope teaching, mankind is actually very aware of these truths, but according to the Scriptures chooses to engage in self deceit by consciously suppressing or distorting this awareness.

The proclamation of the gospel, therefore, incorporates – yet simultaneously builds upon – existing revelation. The gospel does not render null and void our responsibility to respond to existing revelation. In Christ God simply addresses the existing revelation which mankind is presently suppressing.

To suggest, therefore, that unevangelised peoples cannot be accused of rejecting the gospel since they have never been informed about it, has an appearance of validity only if we wrench the good news of pardon away from the doctrine of sin. But this is precisely what the gospel cannot be limited to. Conviction of sin does not happen because we believe that Jesus of Nazareth died on the cross. Rather we are convicted of sin because we admit that what Jesus says about us is true. And in the last analysis Jesus is not telling us anything which we do not already know, and for which we do not already stand condemned.

Thus the notion that it is impossible to reject the claims of

Christ if one has not even heard of Christ evidences a simplicity which spiritual reality does not admit of. As has already been pointed out, when a person suppresses the truth of God he is simultaneously suppressing the truth of the gospel. God the Son is not saying anything different from, or demanding anything less than, God the Father.

Indeed people's belief systems can involve a rejection of biblical and gospel truths at various levels. Unevangelised Marxists or atheists, for example, are already committed to a network of beliefs within which is contained a wholesale rejection of the Christian worldview.

It could well be objected at this point that while all the above is indeed true it still does not provide a response to the fact that some people do not actually hear of the redeeming work of Christ. Is it not unjust of God to condemn those who while being guilty of sin simply never heard of a saviour who could provide forgiveness for that sin?

The problem with this type of assertion is that within the moral framework of God's justice the connection between *hearing* the gospel and condemnation for sin does not exist, and hence the claim of injustice is not valid. God does not hold a person guilty of an additional sin i.e. rejecting Christ's offer of forgiveness, if indeed a person has never heard about it.

6. *Dangerous Implications*

As is consistently being underlined, according to the Wider Hope theory a person's eternal welfare may be secure without their ever being confronted with the gospel message. Nothing ultimate is at stake in taking or not taking the gospel to the unreached. Given this conclusion, it seems quite possible to envisage circumstances where an attempt to take the gospel to unevangelised peoples could be legitimately overruled by a whole range of factors. For example, why should a missionary run the risk of loss of life in order to reach someone who would be no worse off eternally had the missionary stayed at home? Or why should we introduce tribulation into someone's life by their becoming a Christian when they may well be saved without the tribulation?

Precisely this argument could be made on a larger scale concerning the Church in Islamic countries such as Iran. If the evangelisation of Muslims is something non ultimate then why should the Church engage in the risky business of witnessing there?

Thus another main problem with any Wider Hope theory is that one can now find very legitimate grounds for non-commitment to the Great Commission mandate, for example where the risk in carrying it out is a high one. Moreover, if indeed the eternal welfare of the unreached were unconnected to the moral demands of the gospel message, then would the Church not be better placed seeking to meet the humanitarian needs of people in this life? To aid people in their present suffering would surely be a more noble use of the Church's resources than that of bringing a message which in the last analysis cannot add anything beyond peace of mind to a person's experience of already being forgiven by God.

As we read through the New Testament, however, and in particular the life of Paul, we are left with the inescapable impression that all evangelistic missionary work was indeed fired with a great sense of urgency. Simultaneously, it was based on the conviction that the eternal welfare of mankind was bound up in obedience to the gospel message. For this reason the ultimate price of martyrdom was a sacrifice many were willing to make for the spread of the gospel.

7. *Moral Problems*

According to Wider Hope advocates a problem has been identified and solved. The problem, we repeat, is this: existing within society are huge numbers of upright people who would have been saved, but somehow God's purpose for them has been thwarted either by circumstances, or by the inability of God to reveal himself to them. Thus for them the whole redemptive plan simply did not deliver.

At this point the Christian – rather than throw himself into the cause of world mission on behalf of the unevangelised, is exhorted to keep his nerve. A solution, it seems, has been found which can keep the Church on the golf course, and preserve God's tarnished reputation. The means by which we remove this potential embarrassment for God is to erase the very need for such saving revelation at all. In this way we preserve the saving act of Christ as the necessary grounds of salvation, but dispense with any need for moral response or obedience to its claims as a condition of salvation. God is thus saved and so is everyone else! Such theology functions as a grand *son et lumiere* in a world of darkness. A man may not only see the Kingdom of God before he is born again, but may do so without ever knowing of its existence.

Let us for the sake of argument delay our appeal to Scripture and examine the apparent strength of this position. Assuming that this imaginary problem of injustice actually exists, and does so in the terms expressed in the Wider Hope debate, the key question must surely be: does this solution ostensibly provided by the Wider Hope theory possess the consistency which we are led to believe renders it such a successful tool in moral philosophy? Is this argument really as clever as its proponents claim? In short the answer would appear to be no – not even in the slightest. Indeed from the standpoint of justice (defined as a retributory and distributive principle of treating all men fairly before the law) this theory appears to have more problems than it does adherents. One example should suffice:

Wider Hope theory suggests that society can be divided into two groups: those who *cannot* hear and those who *can* hear the gospel. Let us lay aside every weight and sin which so easily entangles such basic classifications on the part of Wider Hope adherents, and progress to the next step. According to Wider Hope theory in some cases when people (perhaps millions) *cannot* hear the gospel God confers the merits of Christ's death to them. This he does without linking the need for Christ's death to any requirement of an obedient response to the moral demands of the gospel message. Thus a person may simply cry to God for mercy and be saved.

The moral grounds, then, of this person's justification are: that God in his sovereignty has chosen to confer upon him or her the merits of Christ's death, whilst at the same time waiving any other demands. Thus within this theology of redemption one's actual response to the gospel is divested of any moral significance, since within this scheme of things there is no necessary moral link between obeying the gospel and partaking of its merits. We will assume for sake of argument that this position is an accurate representation of how God deals with mankind with regard to salvation. If this were so, it is true that a person could indeed be saved without ever knowing of the person of Christ, far less his claims.

Turning now to those who *can* in fact hear the gospel, a difficulty raises its head, and within the scope of moral philosophy it seems a pretty insurmountable one. All of a sudden the conditions according to which God's moral requirements are satisfied have changed. Apparently that which will satisfy God's justice at one point on the map – that is, a simple plea for mercy, is apparently not sufficient to satisfy him at another point on the map – in places where a person can potentially hear the message of the gospel. Thus according to this scheme of things it is possible to have two people of equal merit uttering identical cries to God for mercy simultaneously, yet on different parts of the globe a different redemptive outcome results: for one person a mere cry for mercy brings salvation; for the other this cry is apparently not sufficient.

But this is precisely what cannot be accepted, since the whole scenario would introduce an obvious injustice into God's just dealings with the human race. In the case just mentioned we have different standards of justice being applied to two identical claims with equal merit and need.

It would, of course, serve no purpose to inject into this supposed situation the notion that the disparity in God's dealings is only apparent, since one man has access to greater light than the other, and hence has greater moral duty to respond to the message. This is the one explanation which adherents of the Wider Hope theory cannot seek refuge in. The whole basis of Wider Hope thinking is precisely the opposite notion, namely that the degree of revelation which a person does or does not have is not in itself germane to God's moral requirements. Why should we introduce that as a factor now?

The very question, therefore, of perceived injustice which the Wider Hope theory seeks to address is answered by reproducing the problem in another guise. Indeed the only way out of this moral dilemma would be to insist that either, (a) in respect of salvation obeying the moral demands of the gospel is an indispensable requirement for everyone, or, (b) obeying the moral demands of the gospel is not an indispensable requirement for anyone. But what we cannot have is some third option involving an arbitrary moral disjunction, whereby two individuals of equal merit should encounter different standards of justice. Yet this is precisely the position arrived at if we examine the Wider Hope theory from the standpoint of moral philosophy. Thus the much touted friend of the argument − namely, justice − turns out to be something of an executioner.

It is, of course, true that the traditional biblical position regarding deserved punishment on judgement day does take into account the degree of revelation people had. The point is, though, that proponents of the Wider Hope theory cannot legitimately introduce this factor in respect of salvation unless they do so quite arbitrarily and inconsistently. On the one hand, at the outset of their argument they dismiss the claim that responding to the object of faith fulfils any moral requirement in respect of salvation. However in the twinkling of an eye this requirement is surreptitiously reintroduced by means of nothing more than an announcement.

Such skill would be well placed if the task were one of bringing rabbits out of a hat. But what is required here is not a presentation supported by an announcement, but rather a justification backed up by an explanation as to why we should permit this philosophical *volte-face* in the first place!

That such cannot be provided without engaging in self-contradiction really sends the theory back to the drawing board. Thus in addition to addressing a problem which the Word of God tells us does not exist, Wider Hope theory presents us with a solution which by virtue of an absence of internal logic cannot be sustained.

It may be suggested that by simply reversing the above argument we introduce an identical moral dilemma for those who insist that a person must respond to the moral requirements of the gospel in order to be saved. In other words, it would be unjust of

God to condemn a person for not obeying the gospel which they have not heard, whilst saving another for precisely the opposite reason. Were this indeed the case then the objection would be a good one. The objection, though, is fallacious. It fails for the simple reason that the moral guilt incurred by unreached peoples, and for which they are held accountable before God, does not involve the charge of being unevangelised. Certainly, hearing the proclamation of the gospel and rejecting it can add to that guilt, but not hearing the claims of the gospel cannot surely lessen a person's guilt for sins already committed. It is this sin which forms the basis of God's case against a person on the day of judgement. Once again, to those who would raise the banner of perceived injustice we can only reply with Shakespeare:

> Though justice be thy plea, consider this: that in the course of justice none of us should see salvation (Merchant of Venice).

That some do indeed experience salvation is due entirely to God's grace, and has nothing to do with any of us having a moral right to the actual or potential forgiveness of sins. That others remain unevangelised is indeed lamentable, but rather relates to the dereliction of duty by large sections of the Church, and not to any injustice on God's part or to some moral flaw within his standards of judgement. Moreover the biblical way to rectify this calamity is surely not to linger in the luxury of the academic world, tinkering with philosophical conundrums, or exhibiting a starry-eyed fascination with new ideas. Rather, the real answer for anyone who is genuinely concerned for the unreached is to align ourselves with the present efforts being conducted by many to see a church for every people group within our generation.

CHAPTER EIGHT

Eternal Punishment: *a conspiracy of silence*

The great missionary and founder of WEC International, C. T. Studd, was not a man to mince words. This spiritual hero whose consecration to the cause of Christ in the heart of Africa during the first quarter of the twentieth century still leaves many of us feeling like 'chocolate soldiers' wrote,

> Some wish to live within the sound of church or chapel bell,
> I'd rather run a rescue shop within a yard of hell.

Studd was not alone in such concerns. The great missionary movement of the nineteenth century was deeply impregnated with the conviction that without the gospel people cannot be saved. Speaking of these underlying convictions Klaus Fiedler, in a chapter entitled 'Reaching the unreached: faith mission geography' writes,

> The faith mission geography was based on a distinct theology of salvation and lostness: Christ is the only saviour and everyone who does not believe in him is eternally lost. This makes all men equal. James M. Gray, AIM missionary and later President of Moody Bible Institute, formulated what was then the general conviction:
>
> a. The heathen are sinners like all mankind.
> b. Like everyone else they are fully responsible to God (Rom. 1:18-25)
> c. The hope of heathenism lies not in itself.
> d. We have no right to assume that the heathen will be offered a chance of salvation after death.
>
> In faith mission publications there are no hints than non Christians might find a way to salvation within their own religions. Nor are there any hints that for those who never had a chance to hear the gospel there might exist some other way of salvation.[32]

Significantly, Fiedler, who conducted '*more than a decade of research*' for his work on the faith mission movement in Africa, records in his footnotes,

> In the manifold primary sources, I could not find any other tendencies than those described here.[33]

Alas, other tendencies can be found represented in today's Christian theology.

Threatening to subvert the triumph and enlargement of Christ's Kingdom amongst the nations is a growing rejection of the doctrine of eternal punishment. According to this view, not only can people be saved in and through other religions, as with religious pluralism; not only can millions be saved without ever obeying the moral demands of the gospel; but in the last analysis there really might not be much to be saved from anyway. Poor old C. T. Studd. All that effort – for what!

In brief, the doctrine of eternal punishment is yet another conviction rendered suspect in today's world of designer theologies. Something else is called for which – it is claimed – will once again shore up God's dwindling reputation. Investing biblical truth with chameleon-like qualities, several popular alternatives have swanned down the catwalks of western theological fashion houses:

Universalism is the view which insists that God will eventually woo all men to himself. How so? Mankind, it is claimed, is endowed with a natural tendency which propels him in a godward direction!

Competing with universalism as a relative newcomer is the idea of ***post-mortem evangelism*** which suggests that in some way or another the gospel may be preached to many after they have actually died. Thus the idea that a person's fate is irrevocably sealed at death is no longer tenable within this scheme of things.

Not surprisingly we discover once again that central to this perceived need to repackage the Christian doctrine of eternal punishment for today's chat-show society is a perceived injustice. Thus while universalism and post-mortem encounters are based upon either the negation or distortion of Scripture, they are nonetheless frequently presented as an attempt to rectify a perceived and apparently self-evident miscarriage of justice. In a word, adherents of these viewpoints are *morally outraged* at the very idea of divine eternal punishment.

Taking as a starting point the observation and corresponding assertion that the doctrine of eternal punishment is out of step with the moral sensibilities of most contemporary rational persons, a plumb-line is dropped which we are assured will bring the matter into perspective. Our points of reference are to be such autonomous notions as *common sense* or common ideas of *justice*. The general idea is that God's actions would never contravene our own ideas on such moral issues as punishment or retribution. Since the doctrine of eternal punishment does go against the grain in this regard, may we not be justified in adjusting it to our own sensibilities?

The difficulty with this line of argument is twofold:

a) It begins with a descriptive statement based upon empirical observation i.e. autonomous and common ideas of justice, and from this observation proceeds to a prescriptive statement i.e. what God's laws ought to reflect and contain. Now to proceed to a prescriptive statement by means of a descriptive statement is never a clever move. It has the same status as secretly pushing a rook diagonally on a chess board.

Whatever the descriptive statement can do for us the thing which it cannot do is explain where the prescriptive *ought* comes from. Why *ought* God's laws to reflect our common ideas of morality? It will do no good attempting to justify the grounds of this obligation by suggesting that it will make us feel better.

Not only, therefore, is this argument putting the cart before the horse, but it is harnessing a horse with no legs and expecting it to lead somewhere. In the last analysis all that is happening here is that someone is creating God in the image of autonomous ethics. What is needed, rather, is a concept of morality which is prescriptive in function, transcendent in origin and therefore well positioned to inform us what standards would reflect *God's* value system. This is what we have in the Bible.

b) The second difficulty with the above argument, assuming we ignore the first, is as follows. The question arises: *are we in fact encouraged from Scripture or history to expect that society can or will indeed reflect a permanence in its value system?* The answer is both yes and no. A nation which is for a period of time deeply influenced by the teachings of the Bible can reasonably be expected to reflect something of God's standards of justice and fairness, for example, in its legal system and accompanying social relations. As the Christian worldview is increasingly marginalised, however, and its influence reduced, other value systems gradually evolve within society. There may well be a transition period between two or more competing value systems; but what constitutes common-sense values, or what gives rise to moral outrage for one generation operating within one worldview, will not automatically remain as a fixed point for another functioning within a different worldview. Whether society having once embraced Christian truth will continue to reflect some image of God within its social structure and relations, is entirely dependent upon the degree to which its citizens, either consciously or unconsciously, embrace and apply biblical truth and values.

A clear example of this can be seen in the changing attitude to homosexuality, both outside and within the Christian Church. Something which at one time was spoken of as indecent and unnatural is now being approached with tentative uncertainty, sometimes open acceptance or even brazen advocation. Gay shame has now become gay pride. The book of Romans describes such a state of affairs:

> Though they know God's decree that those who do such things are worthy of death, they not only do them but approve those who practice them (Rom 1:32).

The above description does not fit easily into the idea that God's moral standards concerning retributive justice and man's moral perspective on the same will generally coincide. Indeed at times quite the opposite seems to be the case.

For those who insist, though, that God's retributive justice expressed in his eternal punishment is disproportionate to the crimes committed by sinful mankind a task remains, namely that of explaining what the appropriate punishment ought to be for breaking God's laws. Thereafter we would need to quantify the degrees of punishment on a scale commensurate to gradations of wrongdoing. This is a tall order! As is self evident, to do this we must know the information in advance, and source it from somewhere outside of ourselves. This quite logically brings us back to the starting point and the need to ask the question – what has God himself actually declared!

Hard on the heels of post-mortem evangelism and universalism is the idea of ***annihilationism***. Once again rejecting the idea of eternal punishment as incompatible with a God of love, this view envisages that God's final judgement will be expressed by his causing unsaved persons to sink into nothingness, or fall into non-existence. Such a belief seeks to satisfy the notion that some kind of punishment is due, yet to avoid the unpleasant and emotive suggestion that such punishment is consciously experienced for an eternal duration. Unlike the previous two ideas genuine effort is made in annihilationism to provide some scriptural justification for this doctrine. Nonetheless the search for the doctrine of annihilationism within the Bible usually begins with an intuitive or emotive rejection of the traditional view of eternal punishment.

Let us now consider this proposal. The core idea is that at death, or immediately following, all unsaved persons are consigned to the painless oblivion of non-existence. The first thing to note here is that non-existence as a consequence of retributive punishment cannot admit of degrees. Now for anyone concerned about justice this is unfortunate. Indeed it is difficult to imagine any attempt to defend a concept of justice which involves the notion that no moral or penal distinction need be made between those who commit a greater crime and those who commit a lesser one. According to the annihilationist view of things war criminals and serial killers will receive the same punishment as the friendly but unsaved postman who delivers your mail i.e. painless oblivion. This seems very strange. It seems especially strange considering that those who object to the idea of eternal punishment frequently do so on the alleged grounds that such a penalty involves punishment disproportionate to the crime!

To avoid being 'hoisted on their own petard' those who wish to fit annihilation in somewhere take the only course of action left to them: they concede to the prior necessity of gradations of punishment followed by non-existence. In this context, though, it is not clear whether consignment to non-existence is a release from punishment and thus an act of mercy, or whether it is an extension of punishment and thus an expression of retributory justice. If it is the former i.e. an act of mercy on the part of God, then why can that mercy not be expressed in simple pardon? If, however, we are to regard non-existence as a punishment, then why the initial conscious punishment of a different kind?

For the most part, and despite these inconsistencies, those who speak of annihilationism do so in terms of its being an expression of retributive justice. Nonetheless by conceding the prior principle that just punishment should be on a scale commensurate to that of the crime, we are once again drawn back to the fundamental question: how are we to know what the appropriate punishment is for sinful man's rebellion against God? Clearly, only God can tell us.

In the last analysis the conflict between the traditional view of a conscious eternal punishment and an annihilationist view of a conscious and temporary punishment followed by oblivion can only be settled exegetically by an appeal to Scripture. It is precisely at this point that annihilationists are at their weakest, and traditionalists at their strongest.

For example if non-existence were all that awaited us on judgement day how could the words of Jesus concerning Judas possibly be understood, that

> The Son of Man will go just as it is written about him. But woe to that man who betrays the Son of Man! It would be better for him if he had not been born (Matt. 26:24).

There is little doubt here that the ultimate fate of Judas is understood to involve something far greater than non-existence. If the future of Judas was to be non-existence then how could this be worse than a previous non-existence prior to his conception and birth? Whatever judgement awaited Judas is clearly represented as something far worse than non-existence.

Similarly, it is difficult to understand in any meaningful way passages where the same language is employed to denote the *everlasting* happiness of believers as contrasted with the *everlasting* punishment of unbelievers. Exactly the same wording is used in connection with both states:

> Then they will go away to eternal punishment but the righteous to eternal life (Matt. 25:46).

Commenting on the tendency within man to deny these truths Jonathan Edwards states:

> It is strange how men will go directly against so plain and full revelations of Scripture as to suppose, notwithstanding all these things, that the eternal punishment threatened against the wicked signifies no more than annihilation.[34]

The need of the day is for the Church to rediscover – not deny – the truth of eternal punishment. What zeal in evangelism would surely follow.

CHAPTER NINE

Consequences of Deception

An Absence Of Motive
Let us assume that the foregoing deviant views are in fact correct. The question must surely then arise as to what possible motivation there could be for taking the gospel to the nations? Why trouble ourselves with such a daunting task?

From the status of *risk* it would surely be better not to expose people to the gospel message. If a person can be saved without submission to the gospel, better surely to leave him in such relative safety than expose him to a message which he may well reject to his eternal cost. The only credible response someone could make to this reasoning would be to seek refuge in some way or another in an appeal to the benefits which conversion brings in this life here on earth. But can such benefits provide sufficient motivation for spreading the gospel? Alas, the history of the Church seems to suggest quite the opposite.

In many societies individuals who profess Christ actually experience more difficulties after conversion than before. It is one thing to experience conversion in a middle class suburb in the UK where such a step might only add to our already existing respectability. It is quite another, however, to profess Christ in a society where the prevailing worldview is anti-Christian, or where conformity to a tightly-knit set of social values and customs requires one at conversion to go against the whole value system within the culture. Given that the majority of unreached peoples today live within such areas of the world, and that many do face these trials after conversion, it is difficult to confer any degree of credibility on the 'benefits now' argument.

Is it not a tall order to convince a Muslim convert who has just been ostracised from his community and threatened with death that things in this life are in fact looking up? Similarly, as Christians in the former Soviet Union were starving to death in labour camps is it reasonable to insist that this in itself was somehow a change for the better? Indeed, it is precisely this type of notion that one would expect to find emanating not from the real-life situations of Christians in, for example, Iran or Pakistan, but rather from the comfort of armchair theology, where ideas can be quite loosed from the realities of life faced by many. Surely an honest person would have to admit that this rationale for spreading the gospel not only has a hollow ring to it, but does little to account for the urgency and focus of the Great Commission as expressed in the last commands of Jesus?

Similar objections can be raised against the idea that we are all to have a second chance after death. Once again, would it not be better to leave folks until that time when in all likelihood they will be more responsive, given the additional degree of revelation available to them on the other side of eternity? Certainly this would be the case in respect of atheists or agnostics whose primary reason for rejecting the gospel is ostensibly a disbelief in or uncertainty about the existence of God. Anyone who presently disbelieves the claim that Christ rose from the dead or indeed thinks that salvation can be found in Islam, Buddhism, or Hinduism would also be better left until after death when such notions would be clearly dispelled.

Thus by means of a process of elimination we are left wondering precisely to whom we should best proclaim the message of the gospel on this side of eternity.

Guilty as Charged: *refuting an imaginary grievance*
It may be helpful to return at this point to a fundamental assertion which appears many times in this debate, namely that the Bible is silent on the fate of those who do not hear the gospel. Is this incredible claim true? Are we really to believe that there are no deductions, inferences, descriptions or propositions contained within Scripture which tell us anything about what our moral and judicial standing is before God, regardless of our relationship to the gospel? Indeed have all these previous generations of marvellous exegetes such as Edwards been seeing things in the

Bible which in reality are not there at all?

According to the Wider Hope theory the Scriptures, by virtue of their limited frame of reference, somehow admit of an invisible loophole concerning some individuals about whom God is allegedly silent! Perhaps, though, a more reasonable person would be tempted to wonder how the absence of any reference to such a group could be transformed into evidence for their existence! If the Scriptures say nothing about a category of people who will not be condemned, but are not saved, then perhaps it would be fairer to conclude that such individuals might not actually exist. Does not the burden of proof rather rest upon those advocating the existence of such a group to provide a warrant for their assertions?

The New Testament does, in fact, describe the fate of those who have not heard the gospel. At the time of the New Testament such folks were referred to as the Gentiles. Speaking retrospectively of those who were exactly in this position Paul writes,

> Remember that at that time you were separate from Christ, excluded from citizenship in Israel and foreigners to the covenants of the promise, without hope and without God in the world (Eph. 2:1).

Or again,

> As for you, you were dead in your transgressions and sins, in which you used to live when you followed the ways of this world (Eph. 2:1).

Now we need to ask the question, is this clear or is it not? What we have before us is a precise description of exactly how people outside of Christ stood prior to hearing the gospel. They were without hope. Exactly the same description is given to Paul concerning the then present condition of those to whom he was being sent as a missionary:

> I am sending you to the Gentiles ... to open their eyes so that they may turn from darkness to light and from the dominion of Satan to God in order that they may receive forgiveness of sins and an inheritance among those who have been sanctified by faith in me (Acts 26:18).

Once again what we have here is a description of those outside of Christ who at that time were unevangelised. Given this description it would be difficult for even the most hopeful of individuals to find grounds for optimism here. Moreover, at the time of Paul's commission it should be obvious that among those just described would be some who by virtue of age and circumstances would die prior to the apostle's bringing the message of salvation to them.

Thus within these few verses we have a description of the moral and spiritual standing of all possible categories of persons viewed retrospectively and contemporaneously. We are at no stage introduced to a classification of people who are viewed or understood in a way other than through the standard biblical division of saved and unsaved. The notion of a group hovering somewhere in between who deserve to be saved, would be saved, but alas cannot be saved would appear to be no more than an invention of the mind based on wrong thinking. Would not those who are genuinely concerned about such issues be better employed by reflecting on the solemnity of the words of Paul. Speaking of the coming of Christ he writes,

> ... when the Lord Jesus shall be revealed from heaven with his mighty angels in flaming fire, dealing out retribution to those who do not know God and to those who do not obey the gospel of our Lord Jesus. And these will pay the penalty of eternal destruction away from the presence of the Lord and from the glory of His power, when He comes to be glorified in His saints on that day, and to be marvelled at among all those who believed (1 Thess 1:7-10).

Surely this passage provides the most credible explanation as to why the apostles were willing to risk all in order to reach the many with the gospel?

PART THREE

Seize The Day

seize. take hold of forcibly or suddenly. Take possession of (contraband goods, documents, etc) by warrant or legal write; confiscate; impound; take advantage of (an opportunity); comprehend quickly or clearly (*The Concise Oxford Dictionary*, 8th edition, Oxford University Press).

PART THREE

Save The Day

CHAPTER TEN

Symptoms of Decay: *the real issue*

Given the ever-increasing and incredible advance of the gospel in today's world it is hardly surprising that a subtle satanic counter-offence has begun. This involves the infiltration of the whole field of theology on the issues just mentioned. What is rather surprising, though, is that much of the evangelical community should be so naïve as to consider as valid, viewpoints and perspectives on the Christian faith which seem more at home within the realms of fantasy than within the field of biblical theology. Indeed, rather than hail such missiological novelties as evidence of groundbreaking advance within Christian theology, would it not be wiser to perceive these ideas as symptoms of a spiritual decay evident here in western evangelicalism?

A recent poll of professing evangelical Christians in the USA indicated the following statistics in response to the question as to whether or not they agree with the statement – 'God will save all good people when they die regardless of whether they've trusted in Christ':

> Thirty five percent of the entire adult evangelical population agrees with the statement.[35]

The question must then be asked as to precisely what is happening here to give rise to this type of statistic. No doubt there are many factors involved. However the situation is not original. The book of Hebrews was written to a group of professing Christians who for various reasons seemed very close to making shipwreck of their faith. This was largely due to their inability to exercise spiritual and moral discernment. Their faculties had not been trained to distinguish between truth and error. Although they had been Christians for many years, in reality they were still spiritual infants.

The Amplified Bible has the following rendering of the problem. In Hebrews 5:11-14 we read,

> Concerning this we have much to say which is hard to explain, since you have become dull in your (spiritual) hearing and sluggish (even slothful in achieving spiritual insight). For even though by this time you ought to be teaching others you actually need someone to teach you over again the very first principles of God's Word. You have come to need milk not solid food.
>
> For everyone who continues to feed on milk is obviously inexperienced and unskilled in the doctrine of righteousness (of conformity to the divine will in purpose, thought and action) for he is a mere infant (not able to talk yet)! But solid food is for full grown men, for those whose senses and mental faculties are trained by practise to discriminate and distinguish between what is morally good and what is evil and contrary either to divine or human law.

Strangely, the problem here of not understanding and remaining focused upon Christian truth had nothing to do with a lack of academic training. The deficit here was not in PhD's. Indeed as Professor Sinclair Ferguson has pointed out,

> Hebrews makes it abundantly clear that concentration on Christ is not primarily a matter of the capacity of the intellect, but rather a matter of the condition of the heart. It was not because of the low level of I.Q. that the writer warns the Hebrews of immaturity but because they have become dull of hearing (5:11). It is less a matter of intellectual ability, and more a question of spiritual sensitivity.[36]

Commenting further upon the tendency for many of us to remain spiritually immature the Amplified Bible has the following rendering of Ephesians 4:14:

> So then, we may no longer be children, tossed (like ships) to and fro between chance gusts of teaching and wavering with every changing wind of doctrine (the prey of) the cunning and cleverness of unscrupulous men (gamblers engaged) in every shifting form of trickery in inventing errors to mislead.

According to the Scriptures, then, one major symptom of spiritual immaturity is this tendency to be easily influenced by any and every theological claim and counter claim that happens to be in vogue. Being unable to distinguish truth from error we become characterised by a tendency to be easily swayed in any one of a dozen different directions. It has to be emphasised again, too, that according to the teaching of the Bible it is quite possible to find someone who is intellectually capable yet spiritually immature.

In many respects is not this precisely the problem with large sections of the Church today: deficient in spiritual maturity, lacking in discernment and great numbers therefore being swayed by teachings which would otherwise be deemed unfit for Christian consumption? The result is a philosophy of accommodation which adapts to contemporary theology rather than challenging it. Seeking appeasement within a rapidly-changing society the Church generally has responded by doing two things: divesting Christian theology of absolute truth, and thus avoiding conflict with the world, whilst at the same time investing Christian theology with chameleon-like qualities, and thus guaranteeing acceptance by the world.

The cause of world-wide evangelisation is under threat. Until recently evangelical missionary societies, unlike many evangelical church bodies and denominations, enjoyed a certain amount of natural protection from deviant theologies, this for the simple reason that most people aligning themselves with an evangelical missionary society would already be committed to the need to evangelise a lost world. Moreover missionaries with hands-on experience of and exposure to the reality of the demonic in other world religions are unlikely to be impressed by inter-faith propaganda.

Nonetheless such are the times within which we live that we are now witnessing a brand of Christian missiology the spirit of which is *detonate* with other world religions. If historical precedent is instructive, then it is only a matter of time before the deleterious impact of these views will be felt in practice by many of our missionary societies. Once heretical theology is provided with diplomatic immunity and thus legitimised as a valid, though minority, view its influence will inevitably spread.

CHAPTER ELEVEN

Striking Back

Let us for a moment summarise in cameo form the two facts which have thus far been presented as indisputable:

1) The gospel is being proclaimed throughout the world and the evangelisation of the world is possible in our generation.
2) The *raison d'être* for this global proclamation is presently being undermined from without and within the Church.

To advance the former and resist the latter five positive steps can be taken:

1. *A New Generation of Missionary Apologists*
Within the western world the true message of the Bible is now heard as only one clamouring voice in a chorus of religious pluralism. Consequently the social, religious and cultural context within which evangelicals seek to promote the cause of the Great Commission is a competitive one. As a very different network of pluralistic assumptions takes root in contemporary thought, advocates of the Great Commission will be required to provide not only a coherent defence of the truth-claims of Christianity, but a warrant for the assertion that other religious worldviews are false. In addition to missionary strategists and statisticians who can inform us of *what* remains to be done, what is required is a new generation of missionary apologists who can provide a defence of *why* it needs to be done.

Most missionary agencies draw funding from groups or individuals whose interest is maintained through visits from society representatives, missionaries themselves and mission publications. Very often these same speakers are invited to Bible Colleges, university gatherings and other functions. However, unlike twenty years ago one can no longer afford to interact on the subject of missiology without confronting our contemporary religious culture, which simply denies the validity of the Great Commission mandate itself. We need to grasp the fact that the key question in the minds of many is not, 'Do we still need more labourers?' or, 'Is the missionary task not just about completed?' but rather, 'Is the whole undertaking really as necessary or urgent as we once thought it was?'

God's Word is instructive for us in this regard:

> Sanctify Christ as Lord in your hearts, always being ready to make a defence to everyone who asks you to give an account for the hope that is in you, yet do it with gentleness and reverence (1 Pet. 3:15).

For many years missionary societies and their representatives have enjoyed a certain amount of conflict-free existence within western culture at the level of apologetics. Great efforts have gone into persuading other Christians to get involved with the Great Commission in a meaningful way. Most of the Christian public operated on the belief that missionary agencies were doing a great job, and were worthy of our allegiance. Gradually, however, the goalposts have shifted. A new millennium challenge has presented itself before us, namely that of defending the conviction that the Great Commission has significance at all.

Engaging in cross-cultural evangelism and presenting it to the public requires us to work with our minds as never before. Today's missionary has to acquire a theological awareness, as well as developing thinking skills on these issues and maintaining a key reading programme.

Good missionary biographies can make some of the most inspiring reading for a Christian, especially during the formative years of our Christian lives. Perhaps one of the most thrilling missionary stories ever written was that of Pastor Hsi, the Chinese Confucian scholar who after being converted to Christ took to himself the name *Conqueror of Demons*. The lifestory of Hudson Taylor would also surely be in this category. Next to the Bible, the five-hundred-page biography of Adoniram Judson, pioneer missionary to Burma, is to date the greatest and most inspiring book I have ever read.

Yet while it must be acknowledged that biographies and testimonies of God's dealings in people's lives make wonderful reading, something more is required as a staple part of our literary diet as Christians. We need to be informed and equipped in order to 'give a defence' of our faith in today's pluralistic climate. We very much need to get back to theological basics. Understanding what the Word of God has to say about the holiness of God, for example, or the doctrine of man as a religious being, is critical at this time in missionary history.

Modern religious thinkers have said much about the rights and expectations of mankind before God. The claims of the gospel, we are told, do not sit well on the shoulders of contemporary scholars of comparative religion. A sense of the awesome holiness and majesty of God is all but absent in this approach. In modern theology God is small and man is great. The Great Commission mandate, though, is predicated upon precisely the opposite premise. Indeed, every presentation of the gospel message should surely begin by making the listeners aware of the nature and character of the God who has been sinned against. It is only against the backdrop of this theological emphasis that the Great Commission can be properly presented.

In recent years great advance has been made in the development of such disciplines as cultural anthropology, coupled with an increased awareness of the ethnic diversity of peoples. These studies have proved most helpful in the training and preparation of missionaries. However, ethnic and cultural expertise were never intended to replace the need to have a firm, unshakeable grasp of God's Word and its unchanging truth. Without a confident knowledge of biblical doctrine and teaching we simply have no message to share.

Historically, interdenominational missionary societies have been strong on Christian piety, zeal and personal devotion. Positively, this can be traced back to visionary enthusiasm for being 'doers of the Word', and getting on with the task of reaching the lost. Nonetheless in today's post-modern climate we are experiencing shifting sands in the world of theology and mission. 'Being ready' to give a coherent defence of the Great Commission mandate, both positively in terms of biblical truth, and negatively in terms of a refutation of deviant beliefs, is fast becoming a normative requirement for any contemporary evangelical mission. The much needed devotion and personal commitment urgently demand to be augmented by a training of our hands for battle in today's post-Christian society.

Today's climate offers evangelical missionary agencies a glorious opportunity to be a prophetic voice once again, setting the standards for the local church to follow. One innovative and powerful way to do this is to put into print very clear and contemporary confessions of faith.

(2) *A New Flourishing of Millennium Confessional Standards*
With the emergence of contemporary threats to the Great Commission surely the time is ripe for new confessional standards to be drawn up by evangelical churches and missionary agencies. The publication of confessional statements which proclaim in unequivocal terms the convictions of the missionary organisation regarding religious pluralism, wider-hope, the fate of the unevangelised and other contemporary issues can accomplish several things:

i) Creeds are prescriptive in nature and function as a protective shield. By stating clearly what is and what is not acceptable to the mission a powerful form of theological immunisation is provided.

ii) Creeds can embolden those within the mission on the very issues where the Great Commission is being undermined.

iii) Creeds demonstrate to the Christian public that the missionary agency is attempting to keep biblical truth at the heart of world mission.

That is not to say that the existence of a formal statement of belief in and of itself guarantees the vitality of any missionary agency. However as has been the case in the history of the Church powerful, public declarations of faith and belief can serve as a great galvanising force when this is the need of the day.

What is often forgotten is that at its inception the era of modern missions was accompanied by very powerful statements of faith. William Carey, for example, set down his convictions in a pamphlet entitled, *An Enquiry into the Obligation of Christians to Use Means for the Conversion of the Heathens.* Published in 1792 Carey's work was an attempt to counteract the view prevalent in his day that the Great Commission no longer applied to Christians! Similarly, Hudson Taylor penned, *China's Spiritual Needs and Claims* in which he outlined the task before the Church for the evangelisation of Inland China. These simple yet profound mission statements employed doctrinal assertions, statistical analyses and declarations of intent.

Central to all of this activity was the conviction that there were reasons, and not simply causes, behind this vision for the evangelisation of the unreached world.

Individuals such as Taylor and Carey were *conviction* Christians and not simply *consensus* ones. They actually believed something and allowed it to become the controlling and shaping influence in their lives. Finding the lowest common denominator within the Church and adapting to it was not their calling. Such individuals changed the face of modern Church history for the simple reason that they were men and women of conviction whose chief concern was to bring glory to God, and this through the furtherance of the proclamation of the gospel.

Defending the Great Commission Mandate is once again on the agenda. Updated responses are critical.

Unfortunately, creeds and confessions seem to have fallen on hard times. 'Creeds divide but Christ unites!', 'Truth is a person not a statement!' Widespread ideas such as these (although themselves formulated as mini-creeds and statements!) are doubtless symptomatic of a reaction against a particular brand of Christianity which manifests itself in nothing more than dry doctrinal assertions. On the other hand not everyone experiences God-given truth as dry and uninspiring. Moreover it is after all impossible for a person to become a born-again Christian unless he or she believes and confesses certain truths about the person and work of Christ. It is simply impossible to be active in Christianity without confronting the need to formulate doctrinal statements. Certainly this is the testimony of church history, as Harold O. J. Brown has illustrated in his book, *Heresies,*

> Creeds played an important part in the daily worship and life of early Christians. To a degree that it is hard for twentieth-century people to grasp, the early church believed that it was absolutely vital to know and accept some very specific statements about the nature and attributes of God and his Son Jesus Christ. It was so important that all Christians were required to repeat them frequently, to learn them by heart. The modern dichotomy between faith as trust and faith as acceptance of specific doctrines – usually coupled with a strong bias in favour of trust without the need for 'rigid doctrines' would have been incomprehensible to the early Christians who could trust Christ in the midst of persecution precisely because they were persuaded that certain very specific things about him are true. Some of these things – such as the Nicene doctrine of consubstantiability of the Son with the Father (adopted in A.D.325) appear complex and mysterious. This fact should not cause us to fail to see how important they were to saving faith as the early church understood it.[37]

Behind the formulation of historical confessions of faith lies a foundational conviction: that the use of one's mind to set forth the teachings of Christ over against the attacks of his enemies, is a biblical way of defending the faith. Not only was the method seen as appropriate, but it was considered a necessary part of the Christian's response to spiritual warfare.

On the surface one could be forgiven for thinking that interdenominational missionary societies would be queuing up to respond to any threat to the Great Commission mandate. Yet the very nature of interdenominational agencies tends to mitigate against doctrinal confessions. Several points are significant in this regard:

Firstly, and positively, it has been the experience of many who have served the Lord overseas that in the melting pot of missionary life one's theological tag is reduced to near insignificance. That is to say, when Christians of different backgrounds are thrown together within a new culture in a situation of mutual need and spiritual interdependence, then relational issues become more important than doctrinal ones. For many of us who have worked in another culture this is a truly liberating experience, and one which is not easily forgotten. To discover true New Testament fellowship with a non-emphasis on the labels of Baptist, Pentecostal and Presbyterian is, as they say in Scotland, 'better felt than telt'.

For the most part this experience of being one with others tends to engender within the missionary the notion that emphasising anything beyond the basic doctrines is not only superfluous, but unhelpful. Carrying this sentiment over into issues of theological truth in a generation when the great need of the day is for spiritual discernment may be extremely well-meaning, but can be terribly dangerous.

Secondly, interdenominational agencies have an internal dynamic which has the potential to marginalise theological considerations. Various factors come into play in this regard. As is often the case, emphases which are strengths in one context can become weaknesses in another.

For example, the notion that each person is pursuing his or her independent calling from the Lord tends to foster a strong sense of individualism. No doubt part of this is simply reflective of our western culture. But within such an ethos the very idea of formulating a corporate confession of faith goes against the psychological grain. Moreover insofar as the dynamic of interdenominationalism is towards accommodating differences, most confessions that are drawn up tend to be structured so as to allow for maximum evangelical diversity. However, what were regarded as fundamental issues in earlier days are now often regarded as secondary issues, about which it is considered unnecessary to be 'dogmatic'.

Francis Schaeffer brings this point out well in his final book, *The Great Evangelical Disaster* (Kingsway Publications, 1985). Our present danger is that over a period of time the truths people agree upon might well become fewer and fewer. Unclear, unstated views inevitably weaken our biblical position. Convictions are replaced by consensus.

Additionally, not everyone engaged in hands-on missionary work feels equipped to respond to theological trends, however serious. Given the colossal workload and frustrating circumstances which many missionaries work under, keeping abreast of theological trends – far less responding to them – can be a tall order. Consequently, the battle for truth can easily be sacrificed to the pragmatism of holding things together and keeping the work going. I recall becoming very aware of the fact that my reading for several years had been primarily biographies and my Bible. Enriching though this was, it gradually resulted in a low-level theological awareness on crucial issues. I then discovered, though, that this could be redeemed by enrolling in some of the excellent Bible and theology courses offered through distance learning. Such courses make it very easy, and stimulating, to engage in ongoing Bible and theological study, even while serving overseas.

The result of these internal factors, then, of (a) individualism, and (b) restricted exposure to theological trends is that many feel ill-equipped to respond to contemporary and emerging threats to the Great Commission mandate. This is particularly the case when the argumentation is presented to us amidst a great flurry of contemporary theological terms and ideas. As a result what is true and what is false seems to be beyond our grasp.

However within the Scriptures the establishment of truth is a categorical imperative. Truth is not viewed simply as bland statements of fact. God's truth is empowered with dynamic, transforming properties. Consider the following passages:

> You shall know the truth and the truth shall make you free (John 8:32).
>
> I am the way the truth and the life (John 14:16).
>
> But when he the spirit of truth comes he will guide you into all truth (John 16:13).
>
> Sanctify them in the truth: thy word is truth (John 17:17).
>
> Stand firm therefore having girded your loins with truth (Eph. 6:14).

Finally brethren whatever is true ... let your mind dwell on these things (Phil. 4:8).

The consequence of subordinating something true to that which is expedient is often that mission agencies which at one time in their history were *conviction*-led invariably become led by *consensus*. Thus a form of fellowship-utilitarianism might well swallow up the dynamic of truth.

Another more general factor within interdenominational groups is that the need for funding requires a broad-based message which appeals to most evangelical churches. This in one sense is unavoidable, since all societies operate within, and draw workers from, the existing evangelical church. Finances are tight, and of course we do not wish to alienate would-be supporters on the grounds of secondary issues. Once again the problem for today's missionary societies is, though, that within the very evangelical church the fundamentals of yesterday are rapidly becoming the secondary issues of today.

Dr. Hywel Jones in his book *One Way* writes,

In the debate at the annual conference of the Evangelical Missionary Alliance in 1989 Peter Cotterell argued that as the fate of the unevangelised is not formally addressed in Scripture and is not decided there it should be an open question in the Church today.[38]

The present problem, therefore, for all evangelical missionary societies is that a conflict now exists, and not responding to the threats to the Great Commission is simply not an option. Indeed, in this third millennium the very existence of a missionary agency which has the Great Commission at the heart of its vision requires a justification.

(3) *A New Emphasis on Spiritual Discernment*
Our young toddler loves to sample any liquid or solid he discovers in his path. The only problem is that he cannot as yet discern what is good for human consumption, and what is in fact harmful when swallowed by him. His immaturity at this level can cost him his life, if we as parents do not lovingly monitor his actions.

The same problem can be encountered within the spiritual realm. Many of us seem unable to distinguish good from bad, or truth from error. As we noted earlier, there is a cause and effect relationship between immaturity and inability to discern truth from error. These tend to be two sides of the same coin.

Tons of theological pollutants threaten to enter the Church – the body of Christ – every day with the potential to weaken and destroy our spiritual immune system. The result can be fatal. In this regard the very nerve-centre of the Great Commission mandate is under attack.

Paul describes a key spiritual dynamic which we can expect to observe all around us in a fallen and sinful world. Speaking of the essence of man's sinfulness he proclaims:

> Therefore God gave them over in the sinful desires of their hearts to sexual impurity and for the degrading of their bodies with one another. **They exchanged the truth of God for a lie**, and worshipped and served created things rather than the creator – who is forever praised. Amen (Rom. 1:24-25).

This is precisely the same type of situation that has developed in respect of the Great Commission. The lie is infiltrating missiology. It is being perpetuated and applauded. The lie is: that mankind has other options and contingency plans in respect of salvation. There is no great urgency, therefore, about taking the gospel to the nations.

The *lie* undermining the Great Commission is presently manifesting itself in multiple guises. All of these guises can be exposed not only by examining their teachings and comparing such with holy Scripture, but also by considering the ultimate implications of such teachings for the Great Commission of Jesus.

Take note of something else about this lie: the contradictory nature of it. Paul writes in Romans 1:21-22:

> For although they knew God, they neither glorified him as God nor gave thanks to him but their thinking became futile and their hearts were darkened. **Although they claimed to be wise they became fools**....

Here is another observation about this lie. It can be seen at work in the thinking of individuals who make great claims to be wise about the ultimate issues of life.

Paul warns us that we are to anticipate this phenomenon. We are to expect to hear the voices of individuals who are regarded and applauded by the world as 'experts' in the field of religious enquiry. They will prepare lecture notes, write syllabuses, give talks and generally profess to be *au fait* with all contemporary issues pertaining to religion. According to Paul, in so doing many will make absolute 'fools' of themselves in the sight of God.

The religious pluralist would seem to be a classic example here. He may teach at university, or appear on television, but his claims seem utterly irrational. He is like a man claiming to have discovered a four-sided triangle. It all sounds very exciting, but simply does not make any sense.

The evangelical Church has to perceive and wisely discern that a process of infiltration has begun which will, if ignored, immobilise the Church in the final thrust for the evangelisation of the world. This process, as always, is subtle and slow. It involves theological spin doctors whose primary function is to provide a veneer of academic respectability for what would otherwise be seen as devilish deception.

Theological ideas and beliefs are not as innocent as they first seem. They are at times rather the stuff of spiritual warfare. There are the good guys and the bad guys. Or, put another way, heretical ideas can be likened to a cunningly-devised software virus. Download it at your peril. Once present on your hard disk it proceeds to destroy or distort everything in its path.

God, though, has given each and every individual Christian an anti-virus software package to protect their mind. It is called the Bible. We are advised to read the instructions, install them in the mind and keep them well serviced. This anti-virus package of sixty-six books from Genesis to Revelation has been revealed by God to – among other things – enable us to exercise discernment *vis à vis* alien ideas which, if downloaded into the life of the Church, would distort and destroy the purity of God's truth.

In the days of the New Testament the apostles realised this, and for that reason engaged in the unpleasant duty of exposing the works of darkness in the realm of ideas, and in the context of social relations. The no-nonsense exposure of heresy, and the down-to-earth language used by these defenders of the faith, sit very uncomfortably with our modern tendency to avoid confrontation at all costs. Consider when you last heard the following type of response to an 'alternative viewpoint' on theological issues:

> But even if an angel from heaven should preach a gospel other than the one we preached to you let him be eternally condemned. As we have already said so now I say again: If anybody is preaching to you a gospel other than what you accepted let him be eternally condemned (Gal. 1:8, 9).

According to this passage we as Christian people have a certain responsibility to respond very decisively to alien teachings which threaten to pollute the purity of God's truth. Spiritual discernment is the skill to be employed; and the Bible is the plumb-line by which we measure other moral and religious claims. In days of spiritual deception it would be helpful indeed if the Church were constantly mindful of the exhortation contained in the book of Isaiah:

> To the law and to the testimony! If they do not speak according to this word they have no light of dawn (Is. 8:20).

Strangely, the conviction that we can refer to the Word of God with any degree of confidence would appear itself to be at a low ebb in these days. As evangelicals it may be wise to recall the Bible's own assertion that God has given us a book which can in fact be readily understood! That is quite simply to say that the Bible itself rejects any notion that an understanding of its contents as God's Word is beyond the ordinary person's grasp, or that only a select few can really understand the message. In Deuteronomy 30:11-14 we read:

> Now what I am commanding you today is not too difficult for you or beyond your reach. It is not up in heaven so that you have to ask;

'Who will ascend into heaven to get it and proclaim it to us so that we may obey it?' Nor is it beyond the sea so that you have to ask; 'Who will cross the sea to get it and proclaim it to us so that we may obey it?' No the word is very near to you; it is in your mouth and in your heart so that you may obey it.

That is not to say that there are not conditions to be met before we advance in our comprehension of God's Word, but these preconditions can be met by everyone without exception or distinction. In order to equip ourselves to respond discerningly to such views as those outlined in the earlier pages of this book, it seems that a number of key truths need to be recaptured:

a) The Clarity of Scripture

Hermeneutics is the study of the principles of interpretation. When applied to the Bible it simply means establishing the principles of how to understand or interpret the biblical text. Hermeneutics is big business. Indeed it is noticeable that a great many *fat* books on hermeneutics are appearing in our bookstores these days. Not all of these are bad, or to be rejected. However, picking up fat books on how to interpret the Bible can be a very disorientating and bewildering experience. And the implication seems to be that unless we buy all these heavyweight titles on hermeneutics, our hope of gaining light from the Bible is a forlorn one.

According to much contemporary thought, when we have a question or situation we need to know God's mind on, then we should ask the authors of fat books to interpret the Bible to us. Unfortunately not all of these commentaries are understandable, nor are the authors all saying the same thing. Perhaps what is needed is a further set of manuals explaining exactly what it is these books are saying about how we are to understand the Bible!

Certainly there ought to be a healthy scepticism concerning the exegetical insights of many modern scholars. Dr. Hywel Jones in his excellent book *Only One Way* makes an interesting observation concerning the treatment of Acts 4:12 by commentators over the last hundred years. As is well known this particular passage seems to deal a death-blow to the notion that salvation can be found outside of Christ. However Dr. Jones observes that what has happened in connection with this verse is a gradual watering down by modern commentators of its truth-claim to the uniqueness of Christ.

Thus rather than clarify our understanding of Scripture many modern commentators only obscure it!

This recent phenomenon, tending to reflect a pre-reformation mindset which abhorred the idea of ordinary laymen claiming to have an understanding of Scripture, is now being highlighted as an issue by discerning leaders. In their volume *Recovering Biblical Manhood & Womanhood,* Wayne Grudem and John Piper focus attention on this issue. Dealing with the biblical view of manhood and womanhood they write:

> Since many leading evangelical scholars disagree ... how can any lay person even hope to come to a clear conviction on these questions? Two concerns that prompted us to form the Council on Biblical Manhood and Womanhood were: 1) the increasing prevalence and acceptance of hermeneutical oddities devised to reinterpret apparently plain meanings of biblical texts; and 2) the consequent threat to biblical authority as the clarity of Scripture is jeopardised and the accessibility of its meaning to ordinary people is withdrawn into the restricted realm of technical ingenuity.[39]

There is thus a suspicion abroad that part and parcel of the spirit of the age is the creation of fantastic hermeneutical devices which cannot be readily understood or utilised by ordinary people. The result is that we are left groping for insights through mediators who set themselves up between ordinary Christians and the Bible. The Scriptures, we are told, are very complex and are thus analogous to a computer manual, or some other highly technical journal.

The Bible, though, according to its own testimony has been inspired by God in such a way that all believers indwelt by the Holy Spirit, from all cultures, are not only in a position to understand the basics of the faith and get on with the task at hand, but can do so with confidence. Things are not as complex as some would have us believe. Thus when the Scriptures assert that David was King of Israel, this means exactly what it says and says exactly what it means. When it states in Acts 4:12 that there is no salvation outside of Christ it does, as Dr. Jones points out, mean exactly what it says.

Now that is not to say that some parts of Scripture do not require more exegetical work than others, or that certain credentials are not required by the reader of Holy Scripture. However in most spheres of learning some effort is required if headway is to be made. Certainly, we must rid ourselves of the notion that the Bible is a book for lazy readers. The Holy Spirit does not indwell believers in order to relieve us of the responsibility to think. Nonetheless it is instructive to note that the preconditions for God's revealing his truth to us would – according to the Bible – seem to relate more to our attitude towards the Scriptures rather than our aptitude for theology:

> But to this one will I look, to him who is humble and contrite of Spirit and who trembles at my word (Is. 66:2).

It is doubtless for this reason that an uneducated man such as John Bunyan was well placed to extract more spiritual truth from Holy Scripture than many will do in a lifetime of starry-eyed fascination with the shifting paradigms of modern theology.

King David also records the fruits of meditating upon God's Word with an attitude of reverence and contrition. In Psalm 119 we read:

> Oh how I love your law!
> I meditate upon it all day long (v.97).
> I have more insight than all my teachers,
> for I meditate on your statutes (v.99).

Now there is a common thread running through the experiences of David and John Bunyan. Despite being separated by vast distances of time and culture they seemed to enjoy a relationship to God's Word the result of which was that they gained an understanding of God's ways. Being conscious of their sinful standing before God as creator seemed to be a pre-requisite to that experience.

Bunyan would have been in hearty agreement with the words of Professor Donald Macleod who, commenting on the appropriate approach to God's Word, writes,

> That is the best, in fact the only, hermeneutic. The only key to the Scriptures is a sense of sin.[40]

Conversely, coming to the Word of God with the wrong attitude can leave us standing outside in the dark, rather than inside with the light.

The notion that the disposition of Bunyan rather than the I.Q. of Plato or Aristotle is a better exegetical qualification in seeking to understand the Bible is a fairly radical departure from contemporary approaches to our study of God's Word. Commenting upon this debunking of the doctrine of the clarity of Scripture Dr. Hywel Jones in his book, *One Way* draws attention to the writings of Peter Cotterel, recent Principal of London Bible College. Peter Cotterel would be among those to harbour grave doubts concerning the ability of people like Bunyan to understand the Scriptures. Dr. Jones records Cotterel's testimony;

> I now realise as I did not thirty years ago that the responsible and accurate interpretation of Scripture is not in fact in the hands of ploughmen, and that even the best of translations of the Bible will not make that possible.[41]

Coming from a Bible College principal this remark seems rather odd. Many Bible Colleges have come into being by virtue of precisely the opposite notion i.e. that ordinary Christians can in fact grow to an understanding of God's Word, and to a degree that will equip for fruitful Christian service. Indeed the whole history of faith missions testifies to this great truth. Huge numbers of faith missionaries from the Moravians onwards have been in the category of 'ploughmen'. That is, ordinary labourers or tradesmen whose testimony moves in the opposite direction to Cotterel's statement i.e. a credible claim that God opened their minds to understand the Scriptures. Certainly anyone remotely conversant with the dynamic of church history would surely raise an eyebrow at Cotterel's testimony.

There may well be a subtle irony in Cotterel's claim that after thirty years he as a Bible College principal is confused about the clarity of Scripture. As Wayne Grudem has observed in his systematic theology:

> Historically false doctrine often seems to be adopted by the theologians of the church first, by the pastors second and by the informed laity who are daily reading their Bibles and walking with the Lord last.[42]

As Grudem rightly observes, it is often within the ranks of those on whom Cotterel has set his hopes that we find faulty understandings of Scripture.

Cotterel's tendency towards sensationalism can be seen elsewhere (see *One Way* by Dr. H. Jones) but for the moment it is worth continuing to consider the assertion that the only way in which Christian people can gain meaningful insight from the Scriptures is to consult an academic elite, or rely heavily upon specialists of some kind, for example theologians and linguists.

The equivalent of this in the world of mission would be the claim that only missionaries with specialist credentials in Islamic culture and history can reach Muslims for Christ. A knowledge of Islam, and an understanding of Islamic culture and history do, of course, help greatly in reaching Muslims with the gospel. Yet in practice it seems that those who relate sensitively to Muslims first as human beings and then as Muslims often have the greater spiritual impact.

To suggest that the Word of God is in reality the domain of specialists is to miss altogether the more obvious and fundamental truths about the nature of the Bible itself. If Cotterel were simply saying that many of us as Christians are rather lazy and do not wish to put time into attempting to understanding God's Word, then that would be one thing. He would simply be highlighting a pastoral issue relating to spiritual slothfulness. However his remarks are directed not to the tendencies of ordinary Christians not to read the Bible, but to the nature of the Bible as a book that cannot be read and properly understood by ordinary Christians.

Presumably in order to know what he has just told us Cotterell would regard himself as being within this group of specialists. There are, though, several reasons as to why his comments are less than convincing:

i) *The Authors of the Bible*
As is very well known the word 'Bible' comes from the Greek word *biblia,* meaning 'books'. The Bible is a collection of sixty six books. Thirty-nine of them, which we call the Old Testament, were written in Hebrew (with several parts in Aramaic). The other twenty seven which are known as the New Testament were written in common every-day Greek. These books were written by about forty men over a period of 1,500 years.

Strangely, when God chose to reveal himself in and through this special revelation he did not necessarily employ any one specialised type of person through whom to communicate his message. Amos and David were shepherds; Matthew was a tax collector; Peter a fisherman; Luke a doctor, and Jeremiah a priest. Others occupied various positions and degrees of influence in society. Precisely the same pattern can be seen in church history where God has appointed all manner of persons to communicate and teach his truth.

Indeed as one begins to collect the biographical material relating to the inspired authors of the Bible there would appear to be no particular and specialised field of education required as a universal prerequisite to being employed in this task.

Moreover, despite incorporating the broadest range of individuals in terms of socio-economic and educational background, there is a perfect harmony in all that is written throughout these 1,500 years. The point here though is not that the Bible is harmonious in its teaching, but rather that this harmony did not require any one specialised field of training to make its comprehension, maintenance and transmission possible.

It seems, then, that whatever message God wanted the world to know it was clearly a message which could be transmitted intelligently by different people from all walks of life stretching across vastly different cultures. Presumably the same can be said concerning those who can potentially understand it!

Once again we are not asserting that the Bible can be understood without effort. That, however, is not the same as claiming that it can be understood only by a small band of elite specialists. Unfortunately it is this latter claim that Cotterel seems to be making after his thirty years of Bible study.

ii) *The Recipients of the Bible*
Albert Einstein was by any stretch of the imagination a brilliant man. Not everyone is equipped to understand Einstein in his narrow domain of science. Indeed as he was developing his theory of general relativity Einstein was reputed to have told his publisher that his popular book on the subject would be understood by only twelve people in the world!

Fortunately, and contrary to the notion of 'specialist elites', the Bible's own expectations move in a very different direction. Addressing recent converts, Peter provides the following counsel in 1 Peter 2:2:

> Like new-born babies crave pure spiritual milk so that by it you may grow up in your salvation now that you have tasted that the Lord is good.

Indeed when one considers that throughout the Scriptures we are constantly commanded from conversion to 'obey' God's teachings, it would seem slightly unreasonable if they were too difficult to understand!

Nor is this understanding to be exclusively discovered in any one particular social circle. For example frequently the *family circle* is envisaged as a place where the content of God's Word can be accurately communicated to others. Deuteronomy 6:6-7 records:

> These commandments that I give you today are to be on your hearts. Impress them on your children. Talk about them when you sit at home and when you walk along the road, when you lie down and when you get up. Tie them as symbols on your hands and bind them upon your foreheads. Write them upon the door frames of your houses and on your gates.

A similar experience of biblical truth being properly communicated within the family is anticipated within the pages of the New Testament. 2 Timothy 3:14-15 reads:

> But as for you continue in what you have learned and have become convinced of because you know those from whom you learned it, and how from infancy you have known the holy Scriptures which are able to make you wise for salvation through Jesus Christ.

Speaking of the faith of Timothy we read in 2 Timothy 1:5:

> I have been reminded of your sincere faith which first lived in your grandmother Lois and in your mother Eunice and I am persuaded now lives in you.

Ephesians 6:4 exhorts;

> Fathers do not exasperate your children but bring them up in the training and instruction of the Lord.

Clearly there is an expectation within the Bible itself that the Christian home is a place where the transmitting and thus the understanding of God's Word can take place, and indeed can involve fathers, mothers, grandmothers and children!

The *church* is also envisaged as a community within which the teachings of God's Word can be reliably taught and received. However once again there would seem to be no evidence that a particular aptitude for or specialised training in complex theological matters was a prerequisite for one's being able to grasp hold of the Bible's teachings. Indeed at times within the New Testament world those who prided themselves in being specialists seemed to quite consistently get the wrong end of the stick!

For example speaking of the resurrection of the dead – which the Sadducees denied – Jesus replies to what they thought was a mind-stopping, highly complex question, Mark 12:24, 27:

> Are you not in error because you do not know the Scriptures or the power of God? ... He is not the God of the dead but of the living. You are badly mistaken!

What a loss of face! Here was a group of people who were so sure of themselves as specialists in the field of biblical interpretation that they missed the obvious and plain teaching of the Scriptures. No resurrection! Obviously the Sadducees were heading for an exam resit on eschatology!

It is helpful to remind ourselves that when Jesus chose e.g. Peter to be one of his ambassadors he selected an ordinary fisherman who lacked any formal theological training. Yet as we follow the life of Peter we trace an astonishing growth and development in his understanding of spiritual matters. He became a leader within the New Testament Church, and also the inspired author of two New Testament epistles. Indeed the first four chapters of the Acts of the Apostles depict Peter as a person with a colossal understanding of spiritual matters, quite superior to that of the Sadducees mentioned above. Moreover God clearly seemed quite happy with Peter's exposition of Old Testament Scriptures since three thousand people were saved in one day when he preached on it!

Indeed apart from the Apostle Paul the key figures in the New Testament had very little formal education.

As the Church increased over the next thirty years or so responsibility for teaching the Word of God passed from the apostles to the elders of the Church. Once again though we do not find that a stunning *curriculum vitae* was a precondition of appointment to the eldership. Indeed commenting upon the appointment of elders in the New Testament provinces, Roland Allen writes,

> They were not necessarily highly educated men, they cannot have had any profound knowledge of Christian doctrine. It is impossible that Paul can have required from them any knowledge of Hebrew, or any foreign language. From the evidence set forth above it seems unlikely that he could have required any great acquaintance with the life and teachings of Christ. It is not probable that he expected or demanded any profound knowledge of Greek philosophy.
>
> It is inevitable that he must have been satisfied with a somewhat limited general education and with a more or less meagre acquaintance with the Septuagint and with his mystical interpretation of it, with a knowledge of the brief outline of Christian doctrine set

forth in the Epistle to the Thessalonians and some instruction in the meaning and method of administration of the two sacraments of baptism and the Lord's supper.

The qualifications of elders were primarily moral. If they added to moral qualifications intellectual qualifications so much the better, but high intellectual qualifications were not deemed necessary.[43]

It should also be borne in mind that those who claimed to be teachers of the Word of God were actually subject to the discerning mind of the whole congregation, and additionally all members of the church were to encourage and admonish 'one another' as a natural expression of the Christian life.

It is quite simply impossible to read the Bible and somehow arrive at the conclusion that only a few specialists can understand it. This conclusion comes from somewhere beyond the Bible itself.

iii) *The Confession of the Church*
The conviction that the Bible is too difficult for the ordinary Christian to understand is not only a conviction at loggerheads with the Bible's authors, audience, and own internal claims. It is also quite out of step with the testimony of the Church itself.

Now the testimony and history of the Church do reveal that the contents of Christian theology can involve a life-long study. But once again this is not the same as suggesting that Christian theology is a field of study accessible to only a select few. Nor does it mean that in order to know that some claim about Christianity is true we need to be able to explain the relationship of that claim to every other field of knowledge.

However, if it were the case that great numbers of Christian teachers down through the ages were testifying to the lack of clarity in the Bible; and that this group consisted of the very cream of Christian thinkers over two thousand years; and that the only individuals who insisted on the clarity of the Scriptures were uneducated masses, then perhaps we would want to look again at Cotterel's argument. Perhaps we would discover that the insistence upon the clarity of the Bible was nothing more than a veiled anti-intellectualism.

However, let it be stated quite emphatically that this is not the testimony of the Church. As far as brilliant thinkers are concerned quite the opposite is true. Consider the words of Professor Donald Macleod in his book, *A Faith to Live By*:

> The Bible has clarity. This is of enormous importance. Indeed it was one of the great achievements of the Reformation to give the Bible back to the people, stressing that 'not only the learned but the unlearned, in due use of ordinary means' could attain to a sufficient understanding of the Scriptures (Westminster Confession 1:VII). Today we need to get back to this. The Bible is not targeted at experts, yielding its meaning only to priests and scholars. You don't need rows of commentaries to understand it. You don't need to go to a theological college. If you are a Christian it is for you. Hunger it has been said is the best 'hors d'oeuvre'; and spiritual hunger is the best hermeneutic. If we come to the Bible as needy sinners ('poor in spirit', as Jesus himself put it) then we'll understand it because we'll find that it speaks to our condition.
>
> The Bible then is our authority; and it is a sufficient authority, a final authority, and a perspicuous authority.[44]

Francis Turretine, one of the most profound thinkers in the history of the Church, arrived at a very similar conclusion to that of Professor Macleod. Commenting upon the clarity of Scripture in his *Doctrine of Scripture*, he writes:

> Deuteronomy 30:11, where the word is said to be not hidden nor far away from us refers to not only the ease of carrying out the commandments, but also the ease of understanding without which they could never be carried out, nor does it refer to precepts alone but to the word of God in general.... The question then comes to this: Is Scripture so understandable in matters necessary for salvation not with regard to what is taught but with regard to the manner of teaching, not with regard to the subject (readers) but to the object (Scripture itself), that it can be read and understood for salvation by believers without the help of external traditions? The Roman Catholics deny this; we affirm it.[45]

Gordon Clark, regarded by many as Christianity's most able twentieth century philosopher, and author of some forty books, was another person who did not find his powerful intellect disturbed by the doubts which plague Cotterel. Turning to Clark we read concerning language and theology:

> ... Man was created a reasonable being so that he could understand God's message to him. And God gave him a message by breathing out all the Scripture having foreordained the complete process, including the three stages of the thoughts of the prophet's mind, the words in his mouth and the finished manuscript. Christianity is a rational religion.
>
> It has intellectual apprehensible content. Its revelation can be understood. And because God speaks in intelligible words he can give and has given commands. We know what these commands mean and therefore we should obey them.[46]

The list could go on and on. Throughout history the Church has been blessed with great thinkers all of whom have been perfectly at ease with the notion of the Word of God being absolutely comprehensible to those of lesser intellectual acumen.

The Confessions of the Church also move in a very different direction to Cotterel's assertions. In July of 1643 the spiritual and intellectual leadership of the British Isles, arguably one of the most learned bodies of men in history, gathered in London to formulate the Westminster Confession of Faith. Over a period of five and a half years this group, with prayer and fasting, drew up what became perhaps the most respected and revered document in Christendom outside of the Bible itself.

Now the question we wish to ask is: what did this collection of the finest scholars of the age conclude in respect of the clarity of the Scriptures? In section seven, expounding the nature of Holy Scripture, they record:

> All things in Scripture are not alike plain in themselves nor alike clear to all, yet those things which are necessary to be known believed and observed for salvation are so clearly propounded and opened in some place of Scripture or other that not only the learned but the unlearned in due use of the ordinary means may attain unto a sufficient understanding of them.

The grounds upon which these scholars would have come to the above conclusion would of course have been the Scriptures' own testimony. Quoting A. A. Hodge, G. L. Williamson's cites the following proof within Scripture for the Scripture's clarity:

> (a) All Christians without distinction are commanded to search the Scriptures (2 Tim. 3:15-17; Acts 17:11; John 5:39).
> (b) Scriptures are addressed either to all men or to the whole body of believers (Duet. 6:4-9; Luke 1:3; Rom. 1:7; 1 Cor. 1:2; 2 Cor. 1:1 and note the opening salutation of the epistles).
> (c) The Scriptures are affirmed to be clear (Psa. 119:105, 130; 2 Cor. 3:14; 2 Pet. 1:18-19; 2 Tim. 3:18-19).
> (d) The Scriptures address men as a direct, divine law to be personally obeyed (Eph. 5:22, 25; 6:1, 5, 9; Col. 4:1; Rom. 16:2).[47]

Contemporary Confessions such as those drafted by the International Council on Biblical Inerrancy on, (a) Biblical Inerrancy (b) Biblical Hermeneutics, and (c) Biblical Application drew together some of the finest contemporary minds in the Christian Church. The title given to the conclusive documents drawn up by this group (1978-88) is the *Chicago Statement of Faith*.

Francis Schaeffer, Norman Geisler, John Gerstener; R. C. Sproul, Greg Bahnsen, James Montgomery Boice and other able apologists made up this Council. All of the men participating in the drawing up of the Chicago Statement of Faith are internationally recognised scholars and world class exegetes. Once again we do not find anything in their Statement of Faith approximating the conclusion reached by Cotterel on the clarity of the Bible.

> *Article 23* reads as follows:
> We affirm the clarity of Scripture and specifically of its message about salvation from sin.
> We deny that all passages of Scripture are equally clear or have equal bearing on the message of redemption.

> *Article 24* follows:
> We affirm that a person is not dependent for understanding of Scripture on the expertise of biblical scholars.
> We deny that a person should ignore the fruits of the technical study of Scripture by biblical scholars.

Thus like a seamless tapestry depicting the passing of generations of God-honouring scholarship we find that there is a common theme here with the past concerning the nature of the Word of God. This is not just a book for the self proclaimed élite. Satan's ploy would surely be to take this book out of the hands and minds of ordinary Christians. He would do this with a view to rendering the body of Christ incapable of immunity to the many anti-Christian viruses which can so easily invade the very nerve-centre of the Church. Without the Word of God wise discernment is not possible, since there is no plumb-line by which to measure the straight from the crooked.

Concerning the Great Commission and our commitment to it there is no need for any sophisticated dialogue. In the last analysis there is no confusion in the Scriptures concerning the task and nature of, nor the *raison d'être* for, the Great Commission. Neither do we require the skills of Sherlock Holmes to disentangle the message. There is no confusion concerning the nature of the Scriptures themselves.

Secondly, then, it is worthwhile noting that a great deal of what passes for objections to the Great Commission mandate is *volitional* in character rather than intellectual. Put quite simply we may say that many people reject claims within the Word of God not because the claims are irrational but because they simply don't like what it says. For example, Protestant theologian John Hick explains why he cannot accept the idea that Jesus was the incarnation of God. He writes:

> If Jesus was literally God incarnate and if it is by his death alone that men can be saved and by their response to him alone that they can appropriate that salvation then the only doorway to eternal life is Christian faith. It would follow from this that a large majority of the human race so far have not been saved.[48]

All we wish to note at this point is that this objection is not in and of itself an intellectual objection. Nothing irrational or fallacious is being highlighted. Quite simply Hick does not like the implications of the incarnation. I may not like them either, but I cannot think of any intellectual objections to this state of affairs if the incarnation happens to be true. The strength of Hick's reaction is thus not linked in any way to some intellectual inability to understand the Christian claim concerning the incarnation. Rather it is an emotional reaction to a state of affairs which he does not like.

In a similar way the significance of the present strength of reaction against the world missionary movement seems to me not to lie in the theological quality of the objections raised against it . Often these are extremely poor. Much of the opposition to the Great Commission mandate is quite simply because the implications are politically incorrect in a world where religious tolerance is the order of the day.

However the real significance surely lies in the spiritual dynamics which underpin this opposition.

iv) *The Ministry of the Holy Spirit*
Given all of the above, it could nonetheless be argued that those who specialise in the detailed study of any book, including the Bible, are bound to emerge with a greater understanding of the book than those who have less time to devote to its contents. In other words, is it not simply unrealistic to suggest that a professor of biblical studies at a world class university may somehow be less qualified to speak to the truths of a book he has spent his life studying than, for example, a down at heel missionary working in a shanty town in Latin America? Surely to do so would not only be anti-intellectual, but would deprecate the results of first class scholarship in theological and biblical studies.

This, of course, is not the first time such a question has been raised. In New Testament times precisely this type of issue surfaced within the early church. Acts 4 describes an occasion when two of the early Christians were brought before the rulers, elders, scribes and high priest to be cross-examined on the content of their proclamation. Responding to this cross-examination the two disciples, Peter and John, provided an apologetical defence of and biblical mandate for their proclamation of Jesus as the messiah. Thereafter we read :

Now they observed the confidence of Peter and John and understood that they were uneducated and untrained men. They were marvelling and began to recognise them as having been with Jesus (Acts 4 :13) NAS.

Now the question is: How can this be explained? How can it be the case that these two men, lacking the educational pedigree of their inquisitors, were able to speak authoritatively on weighty christological matters? The answer is found in Matthew 16:17. Jesus asks the disciples who people think he (Jesus) is. Peter responds affirmatively that Jesus is the Christ of God. Jesus himself responds:

> Blessed are you Simon Barjona, because flesh and blood did not reveal this to you, but my father who is in heaven (Matt. 16:17) NAS.

The christology which Peter articulated and confessed was arrived at by means of a revelation from God. At the very heart of the Christian truth-claim concerning Christ is another claim concerning revelation. People do not come to a saving knowledge of Christ except through a revelation of God. At the time of Peter's confession many folks were expressing all sorts of views concerning who they thought Christ was. Today is no different. That Peter arrived at a saving christology was not due to any brilliance on his part, but was rather the result of God's revelation to his mind.

The situation has not changed today. All saving knowledge of Christ begins with God-given revelation. God must reveal saving truth to us before we can respond to and confess it. What is involved in this revelatory experience? Quite simply, the Holy Spirit opens our mind to understand and thereafter to embrace the saving truths of the person and work of Christ.

This is precisely what happened to Europe's first recorded convert, as we find in the Acts of the Apostles:

> And a certain woman named Lydia from the city of Thyatira, a seller of purple fabrics and a worshipper of God, was listening and the Lord opened her heart to respond to the things spoken by Paul (Acts 16:14).

If someone, then, should ask the question: How is it possible for a person to spend a great number of years working as, for example, a professor of biblical studies, and yet remain unconvinced or confused as to the saving nature of the person and work of Christ; or should the question be asked, how such a person can remain at odds cognitively with the 'things spoken by Paul' — then there is but one answer: God has not yet opened the mind of such a person to these saving truths. Thus Paul can write to the church at Corinth:

> But the natural man does not accept the things of the Spirit of God for they are foolishness to him and he cannot understand them because they are spiritually appraised (1 Cor. 2:14).

According to the Apostle Paul two classes of individuals exist, whose respective relationship to revealed truth will yield different experiences. One (the natural, unconverted man) will manifest a cognitive disquiet with God's revelation; the other (the spiritual, converted man) will be at peace with God's revelation.

What is crucially important to note is the radical discontinuity which revelation establishes between the two categories of people. Biblical 'scholarship' does not escape the impact of this discontinuity. Clearly there exist two classes of scholarship relating to biblical and theological studies: believing or regenerate scholarship, and unbelieving or unregenerate scholarship. A radical discontinuity exists between these two camps. Not only will they have different departure points, but by virtue of that fact will inevitably arrive at different conclusions.

A very clear example of this truth can be seen in the life and testimony of Professor Eta Linneman. Eta Linneman studied under such prominent historical-critical theologians as Rudolf Bultmann and Ernst Fuchs. After completing the rigorous requirements for a university lectureship she was awarded the title of Honorary Professor of New Testament at Phillips University, Marburg, West Germany, and was introduced into the Society for New Testament Studies.

Here then was a lady whose life was lived within the academic world of New Testament scholarship. Unfortunately, Professor

Linneman was unconverted at this time. Circumstances, though, led her to a crisis in her lecturing career. She records in her book, *Historical Criticism of the Bible – Methodology Or Ideology?*:

> About a month after this, alone in my room and quite apart from any input from others around me I found myself faced with a monumentous decision. Would I continue to control the Bible by my intellect or would I allow my thinking to be transformed by the Holy Spirit? John 3:16 shed light on this decision for I had recently experienced the truth of this verse. My life now consisted of what God had done for me and for the whole world – he had given his dear son. I could no longer brush this verse aside as the non-binding, meaningless theological assertion of a more or less Gnostic writer. Faith can rest on God's binding promise; speculative theological principles are of mere academic interest.[49]

Continuing with her testimony she states:

> I recognised first mentally but then in a vital experiential way that the Holy Scripture is inspired. Not because of human talk but because of the testimony of the Holy Spirit in my heart I have a clear knowledge that my former perverse teaching was sin.

She concludes:

> I regard everything that I taught and wrote before I entrusted my life to Jesus as refuse. I wish to use this opportunity to mention that I have thrown away my two books ... along with my contributions to journals and anthologies and festschriften. Whatever of these writings I had in my possession I threw into the trash with my own hands in 1978. I ask you sincerely to do the same thing with any of them you may have on your bookshelf.

Thus a person to whom God has revealed himself through the Scriptures by the Holy Spirit will take this revelation to be the supreme starting point for all theology. Consequently many questions concerning the person and work of Christ raised by contemporary theologians will be worthless and meaningless since they are at odds with that revelation.

A good example of this is recorded for us in an essay by C. S. Lewis entitled *Modern Theology and Biblical Criticism*. Lewis as is well known was Professor of Medieval and Renaissance English Literature at Cambridge University. As such he should be well qualified to comment upon the study of a wide range of literary genres. In addressing the tendency for modern New Testament scholarship to undermine theological orthodoxy he comments upon the deference which one is expected to show to the authority of contemporary New Testament critics. Lewis states:

> I want to explain what it is that makes me sceptical about this authority. First, whatever these men may lack as biblical critics I distrust them as critics. They seem to me to lack literary judgement, to be imperceptive about the very quality of the texts they are reading.

He continues:

> In what is already a very old commentary I read that the Fourth Gospel is regarded by one school as a 'spiritual romance', a 'poem and not history, to be judged by the same canons as Nathan's Parable, the Book of Jonah, Paradise Lost, or more exactly Pilgrim's Progress'. After a man has said that why need one attend to anything else he says about any book in the world? ... I have been reading poems, romances, vision-literature, legends, myths all my life. I know what they are like. I know that not one of them is like this.[50]

What Lewis is alerting the reader to is that someone is claiming to be an authority on his own terms. However once these 'sure results' of New Testament scholarship are cross-examined by another authority it would appear that the results are at best less than convincing.

As has already been stated, therefore, a person who is converted would simply not regard the fourth gospel as poetry. Any biblical studies built around such a premise would be for him a waste of time.

Similarly a converted person who wishes to advance in the knowledge of God will for example be ill advised to invest the greater part of his or her life researching the claim that a real or imaginary document called 'Q' was in circulation within the New Testament community, and provided a source of information for the other gospels. It is difficult to see how this type of study has any potential to build up the Church of Jesus Christ, which one can only assume is the focused aim of all believing scholarship.

The essential criterion therefore for true biblical and theological scholarship is conversion. Conversion is the launching pad for all theology, and in order to be converted, or spiritually reborn, a person requires God to reveal himself to him. The person who is converted will be equipped to understand the Bible for the simple reason that the Holy Spirit of God dwells within him and opens to his mind the truth of the Scriptures. As the Christian is progressively sanctified through the work of God's Spirit this process will involve a renewing of the mind through a deepening understanding of Scripture. Hence John can write,

> As for you the anointing you received from him remains in you and you do not need anyone to teach you. But as his anointing teaches you about all things and as that anointing is real not counterfeit – just as it has taught you remain in him (1 John 2:27).

Commenting upon this passage Dr. Martyn Lloyd Jones writes:

> There is an anointing and an unction given by the Holy Ghost which gives us understanding. And thus it has often come to pass in the long history of the Church that certain ignorant more or less illiterate people have been able to discriminate between truth and error much better than the great doctors of the Church. They were simple enough to trust the anointing and thus they were able to distinguish between things that differ. The saintly Samuel Rutherford who lived three hundred years ago in Scotland commented one day, 'If you would be a deep divine, I recommend to you sanctification.' Ultimately the way to understand the Scriptures and all theology is to become holy. It is to be under the authority of the Spirit. It is to be led of the Spirit.[51]

What, of course, is not being suggested is that one needs to be converted in order to identify the fallacious reasoning and methodologies behind much of our modern day scholarship. Many non-Christians enjoy more of a healthy scepticism on such matters than some professing Christians. Another example of this is recorded in an article by H. E. Irwin, *'Testing the Higher Criticism in the Law Courts'* and is certainly worth noting.[52]

What has come to be known as 'Higher Criticism' – the study of Scripture from the standpoint of literature – endeavours to detect the presence of underlying literary sources within a book, identify literary types incorporated into the book and to speculate on matters of authorship. This approach has given rise to the now outdated theory that the Pentateuch is really a patchwork quilt of sources compiled by a range of authors and redactors over a period of five centuries. As the theory evolved it was intertwined with Darwinian philosophy. The label 'good scholarship' was attached to this higher critical enquiry, while the notion that Moses compiled the Pentateuch was dismissed as 'bad' scholarship.

There are a great number of higher critics who hold tenaciously to this patchwork theory, despite a range of fallacies which render the theory logically untenable. James Barr in his polemical work, *Fundamentalism* is someone who takes the patchwork source theory as the natural reading of the Bible. He writes,

> Observation of hundreds of such discrepancies patiently pieced together over a long period and valued as evidence precisely because scholars did not allow defensive and harmonising interpretations to push aside the literal sense of the text, led to the critical reconstruction.[53]

Now Barr's book is certainly an 'eyebrow-raiser'; however we wish only to highlight the fact that Barr cites this patchwork theory as the natural outcome of certain 'evidence'. Indeed he reminds the unsuspecting reader that,

> If one takes the text literally a critical separation of sources becomes natural.

There is something about this methodology and approach to the study of the Bible, says Barr, which not only involves a scholarly approach to rules of evidence, but is most natural. He is really asking how anyone could miss that. Now let us return to the article by Irwin.

Earlier this century a Professor of Ancient and Old Testament languages and literature, W. A. Irwin MA BD PhD, was appointed to the professorial chair at the Department of Old Testament Languages and Literature, Chicago University. He, like Professor Barr, would probably have been bemused as to why not everyone displays the same starry-eyed fascination with this 'natural reading' of the Old Testament text. Professor Irwin quite unexpectedly found himself caught up in a rather sensational court case, the success or failure of which seemed to hinge upon himself as an 'expert witness' in the field of Higher Criticism. The circumstances surrounding the case should be of particular interest to those who like Professor Barr consider the tools, methodology and results of historical criticism to be natural, scholarly and predicated upon accumulated evidence.

Professor Irwin had been called upon to give evidence as a witness in favour of a Miss Florence Deeks, who at this time was suing the Macmillan Publishing Company of Canada. Miss Deeks had submitted a manuscript for publication which was written as an outline of history. The manuscript lay with the Macmillan Publishing House for about six to eight months. At the end of this period Macmillan published a much heralded work by H. G. Wells entitled, *Outline of History*. No sooner had Miss Deeks read this *Outline of History* than she became convinced that the entire work was based on her own manuscript, and that somehow Macmillan Publishing had colluded with H. G. Wells to plagiarise her work. After seeking legal counsel she brought action against H. G. Wells and Macmillan Publishing, claiming substantial damages.

But how could she prove that one manuscript was built around the other? Enter Professor Irwin, the star witness! Now here was someone who specialised in the field of establishing multiple sources within the Bible. Indeed, if the sure results of scholarship were so highly regarded in the academic world, then the methodology employed could certainly not be called into question. Here was the very man who, by the application of higher critical tools of enquiry, would establish authoritatively the pens of different authors within *Outline of History.*

Thus without realising it Miss Deeks' complaint had set in motion another trial. Higher Criticism was itself to be tested within the law courts. As a method of enquiry it was about to be put on trial by eminent legal counsel, whose field of expertise was the evaluation of testimony regarding rules of evidence.

Thus the trial began.

Professor Irwin's own testimony began with establishing his expertise in the field of the study of documents, with particular reference to the type of problem being confronted by the court at this time. His method of enquiry for establishing multiple or single authors and sources of the Pentateuch was precisely the same method he would apply to his study of H. G. Wells' book, *Outline of History.*

In addition to his oral testimony Professor Irwin submitted in writing a sixty page statement of his findings and the reasons thereof. His conclusion was that the book by H. G. Wells was certainly a work which had been based upon and built around the manuscript of Miss Deeks. By the application of the rules of Higher Criticism he claimed to establish very definitively and beyond doubt that as H. G. Wells was writing his *Outline of History* he had to hand Miss Deeks' manuscript, referred to it repeatedly, and that his own finished work was no more than a disguised copy of her original work. Professor Irwin and Miss Deeks rested their case at this point. But with what result?

As the learned trial judge, the Honourable Mr. Justice Raney, reported in the Ontario Law Reports, 1931, at page 828:

> If I were to accept Professor Irwin's evidence and argument, there would only remain for my consideration the legal questions involved in the piracy of a non-copyright manuscript. But the extracts which I have quoted and the other scores of pages of Professor Irwin's memorandum are just solemn nonsense. His comparisons are without significance, and his argument and conclusions are alike puerile. Like Gratiano, Professor Irwin spoke 'an infinite deal of nothing'. His reasons are not even two grains of wheat hidden in two bushels of chaff. They are not reasons at all.

The case was dismissed.

Undeterred by this dismissal Miss Deeks, armed with Professor Irwin's 'expert' testimony, appealed. Four appeal judges sat at the hearing. All four agreed to uphold the previous ruling. One of these judges, the Hon. Mr. Justice Riddell, commented as did the previous judge on the value of the evidence,

> I have no hesitation in agreeing with the learned trial judge in the utter worthlessness of this kind of evidence. It is almost an insult to common sense.

Now we should mark very carefully how this methodology of Higher Criticism was evaluated by those best equipped to ascertain its worth as a tool for establishing 'sure results'. The legal minds referred to it in the following ways:

> 'solemn nonsense'
> 'almost an insult to common sense'
> 'utter worthlessness of this type of evidence'
> 'no reasons at all.'

To those whose minds were finely tuned on legal matters Professor Irwin's observations – far from representing a 'natural' reading of the book, seemed to be nothing more than fantastic speculation.

Incredulously a further appeal was launched to the Lords of the Privy Council, the highest Tribunal of Justice, and the court of last resort in the British Empire. Once again the unanimous judgement of the court was a rejection of the appeal.

What is often established as the 'sure results' of scholarship, as evidenced here and in the C. S. Lewis example, is not as self-evident as the proponents of such would have us believe. One does not need to be a believing Christian to see this.

It is worth noting, though, a delicate balancing factor which will help us avoid extremes. It is imperative that we recognise that the indwelling of the Holy Spirit and the revelatory nature of spiritual truth, ought not to serve as an excuse for lazy minds. Throughout the twentieth century there has been in many evangelical circles an anti-intellectualism which has deprecated scholarship *per-se,* playing on the emotive assumption that there is something intrinsically suspect about any intellectual defence of the Christian faith. However, significantly it was Peter himself who exhorted the early Church to engage intellectually with the surrounding culture in defence of Christian truth claims:

> But in your hearts set apart Christ as Lord. Always be prepared to give an answer to everyone who asks you to give the reason for the hope that you have. But do this with gentleness and respect (1 Pet. 3:15).

Some time ago a popular little chorus, which has since dropped out of circulation, was doing the rounds of evangelical churches The wording was along the following lines, and apparently was addressing the topic of Christian assurance. It went something like this:

> 'I know, I know, I know,
> I don't know how I know,
> I just know I know, I know.'

This type of approach Peter certainly did not have in mind when he exhorted the followers of Christ to provide a rational defence of Christian revelation. The doctrine of saving revelation through the Holy Spirit should be a springboard for scholarship, not an excuse to abdicate on the issue. Empty minds are not the same as minds increasing in the knowledge of God.

The Holy Spirit has been given by God to help us in the renewal of our minds by diligent study of Holy Scripture. In Psalm 119:130 we see the fruits of such study in the life of the psalmist:

> The entrance of your word gives light;
> It gives understanding to the simple.

Thus any true understanding of God and his ways begins with a revelation of God concerning Christ as Saviour. This understanding increases through the application of our minds to Holy Scripture, under the illuminating influence of the Holy Spirit. The call is for a new emphasis on spiritual discernment. This discernment requires an understanding of the Word of God, not simply as a textbook, but rather as a powerful God-given revelation of spiritual laws. The prerequisites for such understanding are in themselves ethical and spiritual rather than academic.

b. Willingness for Conflict

Alongside the clarity of Scripture there has to be a willingness for conflict. Conflict and discernment cannot be separated. Within the western world we are simply not used to the idea that the Christian faith involves unpleasant interface with the world around us. Most of us do not like the idea of dealing with conflict.

Allow me to return to my little son, Nathan. Another of his traits at this stage in his young life is that he regards everyone as a friend! Never having known hurt in life, Nathan does not yet realise that the world is a place of potential conflict. However, like most people he will gradually mature in this regard, and we trust will prefer peace to conflict.

Having an appetite or liking for conflict is not a good sign. Sadly, though, it is possible to meet pastors, missionaries and individual Christians for whom conflict is a preferred option. There are people who seem to feel quite out of place in a fellowship setting when there are no interpersonal disputes raging. They seem less secure when everyone is living in harmony. Possibly it is the resultant expectation that they contribute positively to the fellowship, rather than discussing people's shortcoming, which caused such discomfort. Some people are more at home with tensions than with harmony.

No Christian should wish or enjoy conflict. Neither should it be pleasing to expose or denounce individuals for promoting views which are false. However it is an inescapable Christian *duty* to contend for the faith, and engaging in conflict over the real issues of truth is often part of that experience.

In New Testament times Paul clearly considered it his duty to warn the church at Corinth of the existence of 'false apostles'. Here were people who claimed an authority, which they did not in fact have, to speak on spiritual matters. Clearly Paul understands Christian leadership as incorporating the duty of cross-examining and thereafter publicly calling into question the *office* and *credentials* of these self-appointed experts or super-apostles:

> For such men are false apostles, deceitful workmen, disguising themselves as apostles of Christ. And no wonder, for even Satan disguises himself as an angel of light. So it is not strange if his servants also disguise themselves as servants of righteousness (2 Cor. 11:13, 14).

At times he dug deeper to expose the actual *motives* of those whose insidious influence he sought to oppose. Speaking of the 'theology wars' taking place within the Galatian churches Paul firstly engages in an exposure of the false teaching that has come into the church. Thereafter he fixes the attention of the readers on exactly why this particular group of people were pushing a certain theology:

> ... simply that they may not be persecuted for the cross of Christ.

Was this ungracious and unloving of Paul? Censorious? No. He was quite simply being a faithful shepherd to the flock.

Sometimes he actually names *individuals* of whom the reader was to take note. Hymenaeus and Alexander (1 Tim. 1:20); Demas (2 Tim. 4:10) and Alexander the coppersmith (1 Tim. 4:14). The list could go on, as could the examples of down-to-earth, no-nonsense language used by the apostles in their defence of the faith.

Clearly, in New Testament times Christian leadership involved a willingness for conflict, and this readiness to courageously stand for truth against error was a moral requirement. Responding to dangerous people, or spiritually contaminating ideas like an ostrich or a chameleon was simply not on the agenda. Once again let it be stressed that no one should enjoy conflict. But the idea of a hymn-singing but conflict-free existence is simply not an accurate reflection of the Christian life as we find it within Scripture.

There may well be several reasons as to why many contemporary Christian leaders shy away from conflict in the realm of ideas. As we already noted, one modern trend within Christian circles has been the tendency to view Christian theology as the exclusive domain of the 'scholar'. And, as happens within most academic disciplines, a common bond or vocational camaraderie and mutual respect are easily struck up with fellow specialists and professionals.

Professor Harold Netland, an evangelical Christian who lectures at Tokyo Christian University, provides an example of this in his otherwise excellent book, *Dissonant Voices*. Commenting on his own vocational training he writes,

> I had the privilege of studying under Professor John Hick at Clarement ... It will be obvious in what follows that Professor Hick and I disagree sharply on some fundamental issues, but this in no way detracts from my genuine respect for him both as a person and a scholar.[54]

This is the same John Hick who is associated with the anti-Christian books, *The Myth of God Incarnate* and *The Myth of Christian Uniqueness*. Presently Hick is the most influential protestant religious pluralist. Yet it would appear that Professor Hick's educational pedigree and vocational identity provide a degree of acceptance and overarching sense of affinity not dissimilar to that provided by the old school tie.

Within the world of scholarship it is deeply tempting to allow this vocational identity as a scholar to overrule our responsibility as disciples to expose the works and the servants of darkness in the very sphere of service where God has placed us. Unfortunately the title of professor seems to provide Hick with diplomatic immunity from exposure as a salesman of satanic lies. An incredible naivety is betrayed when we speak of the person as if he or she were morally and spiritually unconnected with the views they espouse. The New Testament knows nothing of such friendly acceptance of false teaching, or such a distinction between person and views. Commenting on those whose theology was not dissimilar to Hick's, the Apostle John writes:

> Who is a liar but he who denies that Jesus is the Christ? This is the antichrist, he who denies the Father and the Son (1 John 2:22).

Various comments are found scattered throughout Christian books concerning Hick's testimony to having once been an evangelical Christian. This shift from Christianity to pluralism is understood to be a type of evolution in Hick's developing thesis on world religion – something of an academic pilgrimage, if you like, albeit heading off in the wrong direction. Once again, though, if the Word of God is to be our guide, Hick's condition is not to be viewed as having anything to do with academic development. The Bible's frame of reference for Hick's demise is pastoral and relates to a spiritual deterioration defined as 'apostasy'.

The Bible is very clear on what is happening within someone's life when they turn away from and renounce the truth of God's Word. Such an experience or condition is referred to as 'apostasy'. Speaking of apostasy as described in the book of Hebrews John Owen writes in *Apostasy from the Gospel,*

> This falling away, then, must lie in the total renunciation of all the chief principles and doctrines of Christianity. For this falling away, then, to be complete and final this renunciation must be declared openly so that the person is seen to abandon Christianity completely.... So we can define this 'falling away' as a voluntary resolved renunciation of the faith, rule and obedience of the gospel which cannot be done without bringing the highest reproach and contempt on the person of Christ himself.[55]

If falling away from the truth of the gospel to religious pluralism is not apostasy then we are left wondering what is. Whatever academic garb this falling away is dressed up in is completely irrelevant. Apostasy is a wilful sliding into a progressively worse ethical state by a conscious rejection of God's truth-claims about Jesus Christ. Hick's condition, then, is represented in the Bible as a deeply sinful darkening of the mind, rather than an intellectual pilgrimage within a world of religious searching.

According to the Word of God there is no justifiable excuse available to someone who moves from an awareness of the uniqueness of Christ to embrace the notion that all religions lead to God. This departure form truth to error is understood in Scripture to be a moral issue, not an academic one. Somewhere in Hick's experience he has encountered a truth-claim asserted by God which he has decided he does not like. As a result he has wilfully taken himself out from under the authority of God and his Word.

Not that the wilful rejection stops at this point. God's judgement finds greater expression by his increasing the delusions which people find themselves captive to. Again Owen writes,

> God sends upon them a strong delusion that they should believe a lie, so that those who did not believe the truth might be damned.

This truth is further expressed in 2 Thessalonians 2:10-11:

> They perish because they refused to love the truth and so be saved. For this reason God sends them a powerful delusion so that they will believe the lie and so that all will be condemned who have not believed the truth but have delighted in wickedness.

The end result is a heart hardened against the gospel, yet seeking vindication in what the Scriptures call the *doctrines of demons*:

> The Spirit clearly says that in the latter times some will abandon the faith and follow deceiving spirits and things taught by demons. Such teachings come through hypocritical liars, whose consciences have been seared as with a hot iron (1 Tim. 4:1-2.)

The question may well be asked as to what is happening within the life of a person who, having understood the grace of the gospel, wilfully turns away from it to a place of apostasy. Again Owen is instructive in this regard,

> There is a proneness in corrupted human nature to despise the riches of the goodness, forbearance and longsuffering of God, not knowing that the goodness of God leads them to repentance (Rom. 2:4-5).

Our human nature is simply anti-God, and pulls away from God, especially when encountering particular truths which we as sinful human beings find difficult to accept.

It is entirely inappropriate to allow some mutual appreciation society to form between those who are for the truth of the gospel and those who are so set against it. If we were simply admiring some quality quite unconnected with the battle for the truth of God, then that would be another matter. But when someone has dedicated his life to casting down the claims of Jesus as the Christ of God and the only saviour and mediator for a lost world, then the notion of cordial respect does not apply. As Jesus made perfectly clear in Luke 11:23,

> He who is not with me is against me.

Certainly, such people need our prayers. However as responsible ambassadors for Christ we must appraise people's relationship to the truth as well as valuing them as human beings. This is particularly so in a generation where the claims of 'neutral' and 'objective' scholarship have functioned as a fairly successful Trojan horse for well over a hundred years.

Given the increasing tendency for the Great Commission to be undermined within the market place of competing ideas it seems that what is urgently needed are men and women who, like the men of Issachar,

> ... understood the times and knew what Israel ought to do.

Understanding, though, brings with it responsibility. Engaging in the present conflict on behalf of the Great Commission mandate seems quite unavoidable for evangelical missionary societies at this stage in church history. A hundred years ago taking the gospel to other religious cultures was not called into question. Doing so was even admired by the general public. Today's climate is very different. Advancing the Great Commission is counter-culture and often perceived as offensive on our pluralistic planet. Engaging in conflict is thus becoming unavoidable.

CONCLUSION

Asking the Right Questions

Twenty years is a long time. Remembering someone's few words of exhortation from twenty years ago is a tall order. Yet twenty years on these words remain etched on my mind. The speaker was a Bible College principal with WEC International in Ghana. I was only twenty two years old, and attending the graduation class of the missionary training college I was attending in the UK. Bill Chapman did not immediately capture my attention. But he turned out to be an impressive disciple of Christ. His enthralling question to all of us as a student body was quite simply this,

Are you a trained person, or simply an informed person?

Mr. Chapman was driving at the fact that it is one thing to be cognisant with the statements and claims of the Bible, but it is quite another to experience these truths as powerful shaping forces in our lives, yielding to them, allowing them to change our value system and reshape our aspirations and priorities. Many of us seem to be informed about Christianity, but trained in the ways and value system of the surrounding culture.

This was the thing about Principal Chapman. He always seemed to be asking the right questions. Not all of us do. How many of us have asked concerning some involvement required of us, '*What's in it for me*?' This is the big question being asked by our present generation. It is being asked in so many ways in a culture saturated in a pleasure-orientated value system. Even as Christians we ask this question all too often. How else can we explain the millions of dollars being poured into such hedonistic ventures as Christian fun parks with luxurious state-of-the-art hotel, shopping and holiday facilities?[56] What other explanation could be given for the yuppie lifestyle and obscene amounts of money being demanded by well-known signs and wonders speakers, whose conditions for 'ministering' in the UK seem to involve first class flights, accommodation in five star hotels and five figure expenses!

Mark Haville, who was involved in the signs and wonders movement for years, writes:

> One incident that really brought it home to me was when the American faith teacher Frederick K. C. Price held a seminar in London at £25 per ticket. People were encouraged to 'sow' £500 into his ministry whilst he sat on the stage wearing a suit and shoes I knew to be worth thousands of dollars. I had previously worked for a Paris designer company and I know £1,000 shoes when I see them.[57]

Here we witness the emergence of 'designer evangelicals': people who are informed about the claims of Christian discipleship, but trained in the ways of hedonism.

It is reflective of this state of affairs that some of our contemporary missions literature is worded to accommodate such hedonism. Bold proclamations that giving of oneself to world mission can be 'fulfilling' or 'a wonderful experience' have a subliminal influence which promotes the idea that world mission exists to offer us the chance to discover ourselves, or the world, while serving God. It may well happen that we see more of the world, or get to know ourselves better while serving God overseas, but this type of motivation will not encourage an attitude of self-sacrifice when the chips are down. There are simply times in Christian service, or indeed the Christian life, when there is absolutely nothing in it for the Christian this side of eternity except the cross.

Only the doctrine of the cross properly understood and applied can function as a basis for an evangelical philosophy of ministry.

A. W. Tozer has summed up much of our 'designer culture' accurately:

> If I see aright, the cross of popular evangelism is not the cross of the New Testament. It is rather, a new bright ornament upon a bosom of a self assured and carnal Christianity. The old cross slew men; the new cross entertains them. The old cross condemned; the old cross destroyed confidence in the flesh; the new cross encourages it.[58]

Making The Right Response

The underlying thesis of this book is the suggestion that a real commitment to the evangelisation of the world is not something which can be treated as a spiritual phenomenon separate from the overall condition of the Church. Concern for the heartbeat of God for the remaining unreached peoples of our world will be evident in any fellowship with a serious perspective on discipleship. Radical commitment to the Great Commission mandate is the inevitable fruit of walking with the Lord.

Some time ago I was engaged in conversation with several Mormons who had started to come around our local church. Some of these young men greatly impressed me by their commitment. While they tramped the streets as foot-soldiers of a false gospel, many of us Christians studiously avoided any spiritual conversation with our neighbours. Meeting together as Christians for a 'gospel service' can at times be an embarrassment when few of us bother to invite unconverted people.

A number of years ago there was in circulation a letter which was an experience in itself to read. It is worth reprinting. The evangelist Billy Graham first drew this letter to the attention of the Christian public. Keith Green incorporated it into his stirring pamphlet entitled 'Total Commitment', published by Last Days Ministries. The letter was written by a Marxist who had been converted to communism while studying in Mexico. The purpose of the letter was to explain to his fiancée why he must break off their engagement:

> We communists have a high casualty rate. We're the ones who get slandered and ridiculed and fired from our jobs and in every other way made as uncomfortable as possible. A certain percentage of us get killed or imprisoned. We live in virtual poverty. We turn back to the Party every penny we have beyond what is absolutely necessary to keep us alive. We Communists don't have time or money for many movies or concerts or T-bone steaks or decent homes and new cars. We've been described as fanatics. We are fanatics! Our lives are dominated by one great overshadowing factor – the struggle for World Communism.
>
> We Communists have a philosophy of life which no amount of

money could buy. We have a cause to fight for, a definite purpose in life. We subordinate our petty personal selves into a great movement of humanity. And if our personal lives seem hard, our egos appear to suffer through subordination to the Party, then we are adequately compensated by the fact that each of us in his small way is contributing to something new and true and better for mankind. The Communist cause is my life, my business, my religion, my hobby, my sweetheart, my wife and mistress, my bread and meat. I work at it in the daytime and dream of it at night. Its hold on me grows, not lessens, as time goes on. Therefore I cannot carry on a friendship, a love affair or even a conversation without relating it to this force which both guides and drives my life. I evaluate people, books, ideas and actions according to how they affect the Communist cause, and by their attitude towards it.

I've already been in jail because of my ideas and if necessary I'm ready to go before a firing squad.

Having the Right Convictions

The above letter was not written by a *consensus* person; this is the worldview of a *conviction* person, someone whose convictions drive them to action regardless of the herd instinct of the crowd. Jesus was a *conviction* person. His vision, passion and beliefs about his destiny as saviour of the world shaped and formed his resolute determination to go to the cross.

So today with the Church. The evangelisation of the world is possible in this generation. However in order to keep the goal within reach convictions have to be maintained. That God has provided only one way of salvation is the plain teaching of the Word of God. The real question is not, 'Is this true?' Rather the real question is whether or not we allow this powerful truth to take dominion of our heart, mind and imagination. Somewhere, someone's eternal destiny depends on our response.

'And so all who are not disciples of Christ are lost!' The teacher was amazed.
'Yes, all, whether Burmans or foreigners.'
'This is hard indeed,' answered the teacher, after digesting the idea a little while.
'Yes it is hard indeed, otherwise I should not have come all this way and left parents and all to tell you of Christ.'

Adoniram Judson speaking with his Burmese language teacher.[59]

Bibliography

Allen, Roland, *Missionary Methods – St. Paul's or Ours?*, Erdmans Publishing Company, 1962

Alton, David, *Life after Death*, Christian Democratic Press, 1997

Anderson, Courtney, *To the Golden Shore*, Judson Press, 1987

Ankerberg, John, *False Views of Jesus*, Harvest House Publishers, 1997

Bakker, Jim, *I Was Wrong*, Thomas Nelson Publishers, 1996

Bannister, Eileen, *Access Without Visa*, WEC Publications, 1994

Barr, James, *Fundamentalism*, S. C. M. Press, 1977

Bennet, Richard, *The Truth Set Us Free*, Wine Press Publishing, 1997

Brand, J., *Learning About Mission*, Christian Focus Publication, 1999

Brown, Harold O. J., *Heresies*, Hendrickson Publishers, 1988

Calvin, John, *Institutes*, Erdmans Publishing Company, Beveridge Edition, 1979

Clark, Gordon H., *Language and Theology*, The Trinity Foundation, 1980

Clark, Gordon H., *God's Hammer: The Bible and its Critics*, The Trinity Foundation, 1987

Clendenin, Daniel B. *Many Gods Many Lords*, Baker Books, 1995

Edwards, Jonathan, *The Wrath of Almighty God – God's Judgement Against Sinners*, Soli Deo Gloria Publications, 1996

Ferguson, Sinclair, *Add to Your Faith*, Pickering & Inglis, 1980

Fiedler, Klaus, *The Story of Faith Missions*, Regnum Books International, 1994

Gibbon, Edward, *The Decline and Fall of the Roman Empire*, Washington Square Press

Grudem, Wayne, *Systematic Theology*, I.V.P., 1994

Grudem, Wayne and Piper, John, *Recovering Biblical Manhood and*

Womanhood, Crossway Books, 1991

Haville, Mark, *The Signs and Wonders Movement Exposed*, Day One Publications, 1997

Hick, John, Editor, *Jesus in the World Religions in The Myth of God Incarnate*, S.C.M., 1977

Jones, Dr. Hywel, *One Way*, Day One Publications, 1996

Johnstone, Patrick, *Operation World*, O.M. Publishing, 1993

Kelly, Douglas, *Creation and Change*, Christian Focus Publications, 1997

Kim, Esther Ahn, *If I Perish*, Moody Press, Chicago, 1979

Linneman, Professor Eta, *Historical Criticism of the Bible – Methodology or Ideology?*, Baker Books, 1990

Lloyd Jones, Dr. Martin, *Reflections: A Treasury of Daily Readings*, World Publishing, 1994

Macleod, Donald, *A Faith to Live By*, Christian Focus Publications, 1998

McDowell, Josh, *Evidence that Demands a Verdict*, Campus Crusade for Christ, 1990

McGrath, Alister, *Bridge Building*, I.V.P., 1996

Murray, Andrew, *The Key to the Missionary Problem*, Christian Literature Crusade, 1979

Murray, Rev. Iain, *The Puritan Hope*, Banner of Truth Trust, 1971

Needham, Dr. Nick, *2000 Years of Christ's Power, Part One: The Age of the Early Church Fathers*, Grace Publications Trust, 1997

Netland, Harold, *Dissonant Voices*, Erdmans, 1991

Owen, John, *Apostasy from the Gospel*, Banner of Truth Trust, 1992

Prophecy Today, Volume 15, No. 2, March/April, 1999

Send the Light Trust, *Gems from Tozer*, 1969

Signs Magazine International, Issue No. 6, 1999

The Bible League Quarterly 1912-82, The Bible League, 1984

The Trinity Revue, 1978-88, The Trinity Foundation, 1996

Williamson, G. L., *Commentary on the Westminster Confession*, Presbyterian and Reformed Publishing Company, 1964

Worldshare Conference Bulletin, 1999

References

[1] Johnstone, Patrick, *Operation World*, OM Publishing, 1993, p.557

[2] *Worldshare Conference Bulletin*

[3] Brand, John, *Learning about Mission*, Christian Focus Publications, 1999, Foreword

[4] Murray, Andrew, *The Key to the Missionary Problem*, Christian Literature Crusade, 1979, p.29

[5] Bannister, Eileen, *Access Without Visa*, WEC Publications, 1994, p.64

[6] From private correspondence by Rev. John Brand

[7] Gibbon, Edward, *The Decline and Fall of the Roman Empire*, abridged version, Washington Square Press, p.3

[8] Needham, Nick, *2000 years of Christ's power – part one: The Age of the Early Church Fathers*, Grace Publications Trust, 1997, pp. 140-141

[9] Kim, Esther Ahn, *If I perish*, Moody Press, Chicago, 1979, p.12

[10] Ibid, p.10

[11] Ibid, p.14

[12] Clark, Gordon H., *Language and Theology*, The Trinity Foundation, 1980, p.140

[13] *Signs Magazine International*, Issue No. 6, p.5.

[14] McGrath, Alister, *Bridge Building*, IVP, 1996

[15] *Prophecy Today*, Volume 15, Number 2, March/April 1999

[16] McGrath, Alister, op. cit., p.106

[17] Johnstone, Patrick, op cit, p.161

[18] Bennet, Richard, *The Truth Set Us Free*, Wine Press Publishing, 1997, p.159

[19] Ibid, back cover

[20] Clendenin, Daniel B., *Many Gods Many Lords*, Baker Books, 1995, p.78

[21] Ibid, p.122

[22] Murray, Iain H., *The Puritan Hope*, Banner of Truth, 1971, p.122

[23] Ibid, p.134

[24] Clendenin, Daniel B., op cit, p.80

[25] Ibid, p.80

[26] *Prophecy Today*, op cit

[27] Kelly, Professor Douglas, *Creation and Change*, Christian Focus Publications, 1997, p.95

[28] contained in *Selections from the Unpublished Writings of Jonathan Edwards,* reprinted by Soli Deo Gloria Publications, 1992

[29] Calvin, John, *Institutes*, 1979, Book 2, chapter 3, section 4.

[30] Clendenin, Daniel, B., op, cit., p.81

[31] Fiedler, Klaus, *The Story of Faith Missions,* Regnum Books International, pp.127-128.

[32] *Ibid,* p.151

[33] Edwards, Jonathan, *The Wrath of Almighty God - God's Judgement Against Sinners;* Soli Deo Gloria Publications, p.347

[34] Ankerberg, John, *False Views Of Jesus,* Harvest House Publishers, 1997, p.4

[35] Ferguson, Sinclair, *Add to your faith,* Pickering & Inglis, 1980, p.19

[36] Brown, Harold, O. J., *Heresies,* Hendrickson Publishers, 1988, p.21

[37] Schaeffer, Francis, *The Great Evangelical Disaster,* Kingsway Publications, 1985

[38] Jones, Hywel, *One Way*, Day One Publications, 1996, p.118.

[39] Grudem, Wayne and Piper John, *Recovering Biblical Manhood*

and Womanhood, Crossway Books, A Division of Good News Publishers, 1991, p.89

[40] Macleod, Donald, *A Faith to Live By*, Christian Focus Publications, 1998, p.88

[41] Jones, Hywel, *One Way*, Day One Publications, 1996, p.37

[42] Grudem, Wayne, *Systematic Theology*, I.V.P., 1994, p.922

[43] Allen, Roland, *Missionary Methods; St. Paul's or Ours*, Erdmans Publishing Company, 1962, pp.101, 102

[44] Macleod, Donald, *op. cit.*, p.23

[45] Turretin, Francis, *Doctrine of Scripture*, pp.188, 189 quoted in *The Trinity Review 1978-88*, The Trinity Foundation, 1996, p.270

[46] Clark, Gordon, *God's Hammer: The Bible and Its Critics*, The Trinity Foundation, 1987, p.119

[47] Williamson, G. L., *Commentary on the Westminster Confession*, Presbyterian and Reformed Publishing Company, 1964, p.13

[48] Hick, John, 'Jesus in the World Religions' in *The Myth of God Incarnate*, Ed John Hick, SCM, 1977, p.180.

[49] Linneman, Eta, *Historical Criticism of the Bible – Methodology Or Ideology*, Baker Books, 1990, p.19

[50] Lewis, C. S., *'Modern Theology and Biblical Criticism'* quoted in Josh McDowell's, *Evidence that Demands a Verdict*, Campus Crusade for Christ, 1990, p.375

[51] Lloyd Jones, D. M., *Reflections, A Treasury of Daily Readings*, World Publishing, 1994, p.141

[52] Irwin, H. E., *'Testing the Higher Criticism in the Law Courts'* in *The Bible League Quarterly 1912-82*, The Bible League, 1984, pp.422-429

[53] Barr, James, *Fundamentalism*, SCM Press, 1977, p.47

[54] Netland, Harold, *Dissonant Voices*, Erdmans Publishing Company, 1991, p.9

[55] Owen, John, *Apostasy from the Gospel*, Banner of Truth Trust, 1992, pp.24, 25

[56] *see* Bakker, Jim, *I Was Wrong*, Thomas Nelson Publishers, 1996

[57] Haville, Mark, *The Signs and Wonders Movement Exposed*, Day One Publications, 1997, p.23

[58] Reprinted in *Gems From Tozer – Extracts from the Writings of A. W. Tozer 1879-1963, a 20th Century Prophet*, Send the Light Trust, 1969

[59] Anderson, Courtney, *To the Golden Shore*, Judson Press, 1987, p.185

Christian Focus Publications publishes biblically-accurate books for adults and children. The books in the adult range are published in three imprints.

Christian Heritage contains classic writings from the past.

Christian Focus contains popular works including biographies, commentaries, doctrine, and Christian living.

Mentor focuses on books written at a level suitable for Bible College and seminary students, pastors, and others; the imprint includes commentaries, doctrinal studies, examination of current issues, and church history.

For a free catalogue of all our titles, please write to
Christian Focus Publications,
Geanies House, Fearn,
Ross-shire, IV20 1TW, Great Britain

For details of our titles visit us on our web site
http://www.christianfocus.com

Autobiographical Information

Rev. Norman Mackay completed theological studies at Northumbria Bible College before attending Glasgow University where he completed an MA, and postgraduate diploma in Russian studies. He and his wife, Alison, served with WEC International for several years as pioneer missionaries in the Central Asian Republics of the former USSR. They returned to Scotland in 1997. Mr. Mackay has been minister of Cumnock Baptist Church in Ayrshire, Scotland since May, 2000. They have two sons, Nathan and Peter.